1/1983

$\frac{1}{10}$

URAL OWL.
SYRNIUM URALENSE.

EX LIBRIS

The Big Beautiful Book of Hors d'Oeuvres

The Big Beautiful Book of
Hors d'Oeuvres

Julia Weinberg

NEW CENTURY PUBLISHERS, INC.

This book is dedicated to those whose recipes are special enough to share.

Printing code
14 15 16 17 18
Library of Congress Catalog Card Number: 82-62408

ISBN 0-8329-0196-2
Printed in the United States

Design by Jackqueline Schuman
Photographs by Teri Sandison
Illustrations by Dave Destler
Props courtesy of Geary's Beverly Hills,
and the Pottery Barn, Westwood, California.

Contents

Recipe for a Happy Author

Take equal parts of love and encouragement. Season well with good humor and good friends. The result is this book and one very happy author.

Each of those listed seemed to know just when to add inspiration, reassurance and warmth, in just the right measure. My deep appreciation for sharing your special ingredients so freely. Richard Schulenberg, Kitty Berci, Serrina Masnick, Michael Marvin, Gordon Bizar, Thomas Jacobson, Sunny Gibbs, Barbara Hauptman, Frances Gelbart, Sam Gelbart, Saul Gelbart, Jay Gelbart, Richard Gelbart, Paddi Calistro, Ernest Green, Dave Destler, Terri Sandison, Carol Castellano, Jerry Silver, and, of course, Mamousha. Very special thanks to Rosemarie Lavin for the hours of recipe testing and support.

Introduction

For some of us, the very word *hors d'oeuvre* conjures up pictures of bountiful silver platters containing delicate tidbits: a colorful array of sandwiches, canapés and puffs in all colors, shapes and sizes. Others envision a casual get-together with but a few well-chosen hors d'oeuvres of a simpler variety. However you see it, these chapters are designed to bring those very pictures to life. For within these pages is *something for everyone*, from colorful afternoon tea sandwiches to sophisticated candlelight crepes. From all-time chafing dish favorites to tasty hors d'oeuvre tortes. From the elaborate to the simple, and a wide range in between. There's even a low-calorie and vegetarian chapter.

Hors d'oeuvres have been defined traditionally as "outside the meal." I would like to stretch that definition somewhat, if I may, to include "outside the ordinary." Hors d'oeuvres need not be limited to small tidbits or the familiar sweet and sour meatballs. Have you ever served an hors d'oeuvre pie or a caviar backgammon game or stuffed eggs shaped like miniature swans? All of these are included here. The emphasis of this book is not only on a feast for the palate, but a feast for the eyes as well. This book is designed to incorporate splendid recipes with the *artistry* of food. For with consideration to preparation and garnishing, the simplest of ingredients transforms into an impressive display. So with spatula in hand, if you will, turn your kitchen into your studio. Combine equal parts of good food and good company, season well with a light whimsical touch, and the outcome will be a relaxed host or hostess, a splendid array of hors d'oeuvres and fun for all!

Take Note

For convenience, measurements are given for dried herbs. Where available, by all means substitute fresh herbs, using slightly more than twice the dried proportions given.

In many of the recipes you are asked to cut the bread according to certain pattern numbers. These patterns can be found on page 31.

The Big Beautiful Book of Hors d'Oeuvres

One

❧ Canapés

❧ The canapé is a bite-sized, open-faced hors d'oeuvre on a bread or pastry base that looks as good as it tastes. As in all fine arts, the effect of colorful canapés is limited only by your own imagination—a tray of canapés at once becomes an impressive collage of butters, spreads and garnishes that delights the taste buds as well as the eyes.

In this section are recipes for several categories of foolproof canapé creations. There are Cornucopia Canapés, garnished with a miniature cornucopia fashioned from salami, and delectable Sea Anemones featuring a seafood filling and egg yolk garnish.

Now to the art itself! No need to be a culinary professional to create appealing works of edible art. The steps are simple, the results masterful. The basic elements for constructing canapés have been divided into four categories for easy-to-follow assembly: base, butter, spread and garnish.

Base: Bread or pastry acts as the canvas for our works of art. The varieties of bread bases are numerous—white, egg, French, rye, pumpernickel and whole wheat are all readily available and thus the most popular. Bread should be chilled in the refrigerator for 24 hours before it is to be cut. This chilling process firms the bread and keeps it from tearing when you trim crusts or slice and cut shapes.

Trim crusts off after the spread is applied. This adds that clean, crisp edge so important to the discriminating eye. Bread is a most versatile canvas, indeed; a different cut, a new shape, creates a whole new look for your hors d'oeuvres. Consult page 31 for various bread cutting designs. (Hints for preparing and slicing canapé bread bases are applicable to tea sandwiches as well.)

Pullman loaf, named for the railroad car its shape resembles, refers to any rectangular loaf, rather than to a particular variety of bread. Since it is whole and can be sliced horizontally, the advantages of the pullman are that it's convenient, saves time and minimizes waste. One loaf can be used to make several different canapé and tea sandwich recipes. Remember, however, that you may substitute 4X4-inch sandwich slices whenever your recipe calls for a pullman. (Recipe yields in this book are calculated for both 4X4 sandwich and pullman slices.) Ask your bakery to slice the loaves horizontally one-quarter to one-half inch thick. Length will vary depending on your baker's pans, but most pullman loaves measure 4X4X12 inches. Finally, to add an especially festive touch, special-order your bread with a delicate tint, such as pale pink or green, to complement the colors of your canapés.

Butter: This edible sealer for our consumable canvas prevents the seepage of the various spreads and protects the bases from becoming soggy. Butter should be softened at room temperature, rather than melted, and is often combined with other ingredients for added flavor.

Spread: There is great latitude in the ingredients. Combinations of various meats or seafoods add taste and texture to the canapés. Cream cheese spreads should be allowed to soften to room temperature for easy use.

Garnish: Voila! The finishing touch. Those very personal signatures to your works of art feature a wide range of condiments and vegetables.

DO-AHEAD NOTE

For the tastiest results, prepare the butters and spreads the day before. Several hours before serving apply the butter and spread and garnish. Refrigerate and serve cold.

Caviar Canapés

Yields 48 canapés from pullman slices; 28 from 4X4 sandwich slices.

A very elegant variation of the canapé! Half the bread is spread with caviar scented with lemon, the other half with chopped egg. Tomato paste piping colorfully separates the two.

INGREDIENTS

2 shallots, minced

¾ cup butter, softened

4 hard-cooked egg yolks

¼ cup tomato paste

1 lemon

¾ cup black caviar

3 pullman slices pumpernickel cut ½ inch thick, or 7 4X4 sandwich slices pumpernickel

4 to 6 hard-cooked eggs, finely chopped

INSTRUCTIONS

1. Combine minced shallots and butter and whip until thoroughly blended. Set aside.

2. In a mixing bowl combine the 4 egg yolks with the tomato paste; blend thoroughly. Fill a pastry bag with the mixture.

3. Slice the lemon thinly and cut each slice into quarters.

4. Place the bread slices on a cutting board and spread with a thin, even layer of the shallot butter.

5. Cut an inch-wide strip from the length of each slice of bread. This makes the bread just the right

SPECIAL EQUIPMENT
Pastry bag with writing tip

Base: Use any thinly sliced dark bread (I suggest pumpernickel). Lengthwise pullman slices are preferable, but regular 4X4 sandwich slices can be used.
Butter: A combination of minced shallots and butter
Spread: Black caviar and finely chopped egg
Garnish: Tomato paste and egg yolk piping and tiny lemon wedges

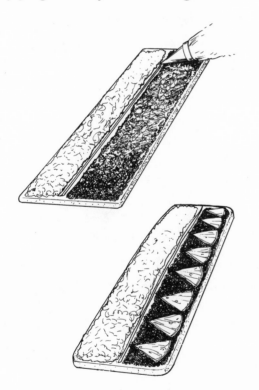

size for canapes. (The strips will not go to waste, but will be used to make individual canapes.)

6. Spread a thin layer of caviar on a lengthwise half of each slice of bread. Spread the chopped eggs generously on the other half.

7. Pipe the tomato-egg yolk mixture along the dividing line between the caviar and chopped eggs.
8. Top the caviar side with the tiny lemon wedges.
9. Cut the remaining bread strips into 2½-inch-long pieces and repeat the procedure.
10. Cut the bread into small rectangles, using pattern #1 for pullman slices and pattern #14 for 4X4 sandwich slices. Arrange artfully on a platter and refrigerate until serving time.

DO-AHEAD NOTE

It is not advisable to refrigerate caviar canapes overnight. After paying a premium price for those little black fish eggs, do allow the time and attention to freshness they deserve by making the canapes several hours before serving. Preparation time is short, though their appearance is elaborate.
The shallot butter and chopped eggs may be prepared the night before and refrigerated. Allow the mixture to reach room temperature before spreading.

Cornucopia Canapés

Cornucopia Canapés are probably the fastest of all canapés to prepare, and yet they provide a striking display of color and pattern. I use an assembly line technique that allows speedy production without sacrificing artistry. Another plus with this eye-catching hors d'oeuvre is that it can be prepared the day before your party and refrigerated until serving time.

INGREDIENTS

¼ teaspoon garlic powder

¾ cup butter, softened

3 pullman slices white or egg bread cut ½ inch thick, or 7 4X4 sandwich slices

16 ounces processed cheese spread

20 slices of salami (3 inches in diameter)

3½-ounce can pitted black or pimiento-stuffed olives

8 ounces cream cheese, softened at room temperature

4-ounce jar pimiento strips

SPECIAL EQUIPMENT

Pastry bag with star tip

Cellophane-tipped toothpicks

Base: White or egg bread
Spread: Cheese spread
Garnish: Miniature salami cornucopias, cream cheese and pimiento strips

INSTRUCTIONS

1. Combine garlic powder with butter and spread a thin layer on the bread, covering all corners.

2. In a double boiler melt the cheese spread. Cheese will be a soft consistency and easy to spread.

3. Spread a generous layer of the warm cheese on the buttered bread. Allow the cheese to cool on the bread.

4. Trim the crusts with a sharp knife to leave a clean edge.

5. To make the cornucopia garnish, cut the salami slices in half and roll each into a cone. With a cellophane-tipped toothpick, skewer an olive, then the salami cone at an angle.

6. Insert the cornucopias on the bread at an angle, in a row about ½ inch from the edge. Each canapé will be approximately 1½ inches wide and 2½ inches long, so place your cornucopias accordingly.

7. Fill a star-tipped pastry bag with softened cream cheese.

8. Pipe cream cheese into each salami cornucopia.

9. Place a pimiento strip on the bread to the right of each cornucopia.

10. Cut the bread into small rectangles using pattern #1 for pullman slices or pattern #14 for 4X4

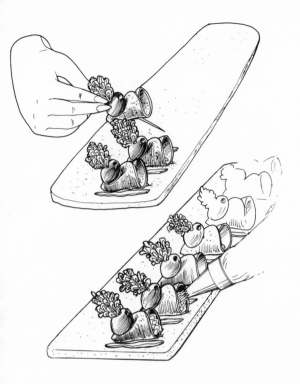

sandwich slices. Arrange the canapés artfully on a platter. Chill and serve.

DO-AHEAD NOTE

Though it is generally preferable to prepare hors d'oeuvres as close to serving time as possible, cornucopia canapés can be prepared the night before. To store, place the uncut canapés (garnished only with the salami cornucopias filled with cream cheese) in a shallow container lined with a damp paper towel. Cover and refrigerate. Garnish with pimiento strips, cut the bread and arrange on a platter just before serving.

SPECIAL HINTS

Each pullman slice will yield 13 cornucopias; each 4X4 slice will yield 4.

Tuna-Walnut Anemones

Yields 30 anemones.

Watch the delightful reaction these tasty anemones draw from your guests. They're filled with a creamy tuna spread and garnished with a crunchy ring of walnuts and mint.

INGREDIENTS

1 recipe Tuna Salad, page 162
2 hard-cooked eggs, chopped
1 tablespoon mayonnaise-style salad
   dressing
1 cup finely chopped walnuts
¼ cup finely chopped fresh mint leaves
   or parsley
¾ cup butter, softened
8 pullman slices egg or white bread, cut
   ½ inch thick, or 15 4X4 sandwich
   slices white bread
2-ounce jar pimiento strips

INSTRUCTIONS

1. Combine the tuna salad, chopped eggs and salad dressing in a blender or food processor. Blend until smooth.
2. Combine well the walnuts and mint.
3. Spread a smooth layer of butter on the bread and cut 60 rounds with the 2-inch cutter. Remove the centers from 30 of the rounds with the 1½-inch cutter and discard them. These rounds wll resemble small donuts.
4. Place a donut-shaped bread round over a solid round and generously butter the outside edges of the two layers.

SPECIAL EQUIPMENT
Two cookie cutters: 1½ inches round
and 2 inches round
Melon-baller

Base: Egg or white bread
Butter: Softened butter
Spread: A combination of tuna salad,
eggs and mayonnaise-style salad
dressing
Garnish: Chopped mint or parsley and
parsley sprigs or pimiento strips, well
drained

5. Roll the edges of the buttered bread rounds in the walnut-mint combination. The finely chopped walnuts and mint will stick to the buttered surface.
6. With a melon-baller, fill the centers of each of the rounds with a small mound of the tuna spread.
7. Apply the pimiento strips over the tuna mound, making a cross design, or garnish with a sprig of parsley for color. Refrigerate and serve chilled.

DO-AHEAD NOTE
To prepare several days in advance, cut the bread into rounds and freeze them unbuttered in a moisture-proof container. The day before your party, prepare the tuna spread. Assemble the anemones and garnish the day of the party.

Sea Anemone Canapés

Yields 30 anemones.

The Sea Anemone is a picture-perfect canapé. In keeping with its name, this hors d'oeuvre looks like it came from the ocean, complete with garnished tentacles. Like a true sea creature, it treats the taste buds to a marine experience with tasty fillings of shrimp, salmon and tuna. It's a quick and easy hors d'oeuvre that can be assembled in several stages to save time. After you've tried the suggested recipes, feel free to experiment with other spreads to fully appreciate the artistry and versatility of this design.

INGREDIENTS
½ pound cooked shrimp—shelled,
    deveined and coarsely chopped
1 tablespoon mayonnaise-style salad
    dressing
¼ teaspoon garlic powder
1 teaspoon dill
1 tablespoon chopped chives
4 hard-cooked eggs, whites and yolks
    separated

INSTRUCTIONS
1. In a blender or food processor combine shrimp, salad dressing, garlic powder, dill, chives and egg whites.
2. Spread a smooth layer of butter on the bread slices and cut into 60 rounds with the 2-inch cutter. Remove the centers from 30 of the rounds with the 1½-inch cutter and discard them. These rounds will resemble small donuts.
3. Place a donut-shaped bread round over a solid

¾ cup butter, softened
8 pullman slices egg or white bread, cut
    ½ inch thick, or 15 4X4 sandwich
    slices white bread
2-ounce jar pimiento-stuffed olives
Parsley (optional)

SPECIAL EQUIPMENT
Two cookie cutters: 1½ inches round
and 2 inches round
Small mesh strainer
Melon-baller

Base: Egg or white bread
Butter: Softened butter
Spread: A combination of shrimp, egg
whites, garlic powder, mayonnaise-
style salad dressing, dill and chives
Garnish: Strained egg yolks and
pimiento-stuffed olives or parsley

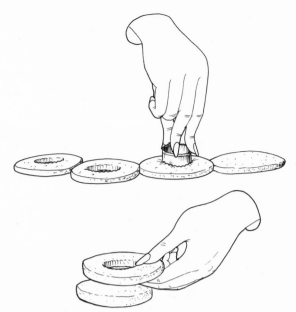

round and generously butter the edges of the two
layers.

4. Force the egg yolks through a strainer. Stir the
strained yolks lightly with a fork.

5. Roll the edges of the bread rounds in the strained
egg yolks. The egg yolks will stick to the buttered
surface. Shake off any excess. Repeat until all the
rounds are covered with strained egg yolks.

6. With a melon-baller, fill each of the centers of the
rounds with a small mound of the shrimp spread.

7. To garnish, slice the pimiento-stuffed olives and
top each anemone with a slice. Serve chilled.

DO-AHEAD NOTE

To prepare several days in advance, cut the bread
into rounds and place unbuttered in a moisture-
proof container in the freezer. The day before your
special occasion, prepare the shrimp spread. Prepare the strained egg yolk the day of the party.

Salmon Sea Anemones

Yields 30 anemones.

Smooth pink salmon with a touch of onion combine to make this hors d'oeuvre. Surrounded with chopped black olives, the color and taste combination make these anemones irresistible.

INGREDIENTS

1½ cups canned salmon, flaked
2 tablespoons mayonnaise-style salad dressing
3 hard-cooked eggs, chopped
¼ teaspoon garlic powder
2 tablespoons chopped onion
½ cup butter, softened
8 pullman slices egg or white bread or 15 4X4 sandwich slices
½ cup mayonnaise
4½-ounce can pitted black olives, well drained and chopped
Small bunch parsley

SPECIAL EQUIPMENT

Two cookie cutters: 1½ inches round and 2 inches round
Melon-baller

Base: 8 pullman slices white or egg bread or 15 4X4 sandwich slices
Butter: Softened butter
Spread: A combination of salmon, mayonnaise-style salad dressing, chopped eggs, garlic powder and onions
Garnish: Chopped black olives and parsley sprigs

INSTRUCTIONS

1. In a blender combine salmon, mayonnaise-style salad dressing, eggs, garlic powder and onion. Mix until smooth.
2. Spread a layer of butter on the bread slices and cut 60 rounds with the 2-inch cutter. Remove the centers from 30 of the rounds with the 1½-inch cutter. Discard the centers.
3. Place a donut-shaped round over a solid round and generously spread a smooth layer of mayonnaise around the edges of the two layers.
4. Roll the edges in the chopped olives. Repeat the process until all the rounds are covered with the olives.
5. With a melon-baller, fill each of the centers of the rounds with a small mound of the salmon spread.
6. Top each mound with a tiny parsley sprig for color. Refrigerate and serve chilled.

DO-AHEAD NOTE

To prepare several days in advance, cut the bread into rounds and freeze them unbuttered in a moisture-proof container. The day before your special occasion, prepare the salmon spread. Assemble the anemones and garnish the day of the party.

Miniature Puffs

These light, fluffy puffs serve as deliciously edible containers for a variety of cold fillings. They are a light and decorative addition to a platter of canapés.

INGREDIENTS
½ cup water
¼ cup butter
½ cup flour
2 eggs

INSTRUCTIONS
1. Preheat oven to 400 degrees.
2. In a saucepan, heat water and butter to boiling. Reduce heat and add flour all at once. Stir approximately 1 minute, until the mixture forms a ball. Remove from heat.
3. Beat in the eggs one at a time until the mixture is smooth.
4. Place rounded teaspoonfuls of the dough on an ungreased baking sheet.
5. Bake 25 minutes, or until golden brown. Remove from the oven; allow to cool.
6. Cut off tops of puffs with a knife. Remove any moist dough from inside the puffs and add your favorite filling or use one of the following recipes with fillings.

Ham-Pickle Puffs

Yields approximately 25 puffs.

Light and tasty, these miniature puffs are filled with a smooth ham-pickle mixture that's softened with cream cheese and blended with garlic powder and dry mustard.

INGREDIENTS
1 recipe Miniature Puffs, page 19
½ cup ground cooked ham
¼ teaspoon dry mustard
¼ cup minced sweet pickle
2 ounces cream cheese, softened
Dash of garlic powder
Pepper to taste

INSTRUCTIONS
1. Prepare miniature puffs according to the recipe. While puffs are baking, prepare the filling.
2. In a mixing bowl, combine ham, mustard, pickle, cream cheese, garlic powder and pepper. Blend thoroughly.
3. Slice off the tops of the puffs and scoop out the moist centers.
4. Place approximately 1 teaspoon of the filling in each puff. Replace the tops and refrigerate until serving time.

Cheddar Cheese Puffs

Yields approximately 25 puffs.

These little puffs, filled with a zesty sharp Cheddar cheese, are mixed with a colorful combination of pimiento-stuffed olives and chives.

INGREDIENTS

1 recipe Miniature Puffs, page 19
¾ cup sharp, spreadable Cheddar cheese
1 tablespoon mayonnaise-style salad dressing
¼ cup chopped pimiento-stuffed olives
1 tablespoon minced chives

INSTRUCTIONS

1. Prepare miniature puffs according to the recipe.
2. Whip cheese and salad dressing in a bowl until fluffy.
3. Add olives and chives and mix thoroughly.
4. Cut off the tops of the puffs and scoop out the moist centers.
5. Place approximately 1 teaspoon of the filling in each puff. Replace the tops and refrigerate until serving time.

Piped Canapés

Yields will vary according to cutting design used.

These delightful canapés get their design from clever bread shapes and their patterns from artful piping. Choose from a variety of your favorite cookie cutter shapes or from those designs offered on page 31. Any smooth spread can be piped onto the bread base. Imagine the fabulous combinations of colors and flavors you can create. Just cut, create and pipe!

INGREDIENTS

¾ cup butter, softened
1 tablespoon prepared mustard
2 cups finely ground cooked ham
1 tablespoon cream cheese
1 teaspoon mayonnaise-style salad dressing
Dash of garlic powder
Pullman slices or 4X4 sandwich slices, white or egg bread.
3½-ounce can black olives
3½-ounce can green olives
4-ounce can whole pimientos

INSTRUCTIONS

1. Combine butter and mustard and mix well. Let stand at room temperature.
2. In a blender, combine ham, cream cheese, salad dressing and garlic powder. Whip into a smooth paste.
3. Spread a thin layer of mustard butter on the bread slices.
4. Cut the bread with assorted cookie cutters or use designs #1 through #6 for pullman slices or #9 through #16 for 4X4 slices.
5. Fill a star- or shell-tipped pastry bag with the ham spread. Pipe the spread onto the cut bread designs.

SPECIAL EQUIPMENT

Blender or food processor

Cookie cutters

Aspic cutters

Pastry bag with shell or star tip

Base: White or egg bread

Butter: Softened butter combined with prepared mustard

Spread: Combination of finely ground ham, cream cheese, salad dressing and garlic powder

Garnish: Black or green olives and pimientos.

6. Garnish with olives or cut pimientos into designs with aspic cutters. You may want to combine condiments, or simply use sliced olive. There's plenty of room for creativity here, so have fun!

7. Arrange piped canapés on a platter, chill and serve.

SPECIAL HINTS

Substitute chicken, tongue or any other meat that can be ground into a smooth paste and piped. When preparing spreads, be sure to grind meats thoroughly before adding other ingredients. To thicken the spreads add more ground meat. To thin, add more cream cheese.

You can use a knife to smooth the spread on the base rather than piping, then simply garnish.

Two

❧ Tea Sandwiches

❧ For elegant luncheons or midafternoon get-togethers, what could be more appropriate than tea sandwiches? They're light yet filling, dainty and delectable, and they can be as simple or as elaborate as you wish. You can combine two or three kinds of breads—date-nut and raisin, for example—and alternate them with beautiful pastel spreads of meats or sweets. Once you're familiar with general tea sandwich preparation, you'll want to experiment with various fillings of your own. You can garnish them with edible piped flowers or finely chopped herbs, but many times they need no extra decoration, because their ingredients are so colorful. As for convenience, tea sandwiches are at the top of the party list. Since they're not open-faced, they will not dry out as quickly, so they can be prepared well in advance and refrigerated. And their versatility enables them to be cut in any of the patterns shown on page 31.

GENERAL SANDWICH SUGGESTIONS

To prevent soggy sandwiches, spread a thin layer of softened butter on the insides of the bread, being sure to cover all edges.

Whip, rather than melt, the butter. Allow butter to stand at room temperature until soft, then whip until fluffy.

TO STORE SANDWICHES

1. Put sandwiches in a shallow container lined with a damp towel on the bottom and covered with wax paper. Stack the sandwiches with layers of wax paper between them.

2. Rolled and ribbon sandwiches can be wrapped uncut, then sliced while still partially frozen for sharp, clean edges.

3. Thaw for one to two hours in the original wrapping, then refrigerate if not used immediately.

4. Sandwiches may be frozen for up to two weeks, but should not be refrozen.

5. Do not freeze sandwiches containing jelly, mayonnaise, salad dressing, hard-cooked egg whites, lettuce, celery, tomatoes or carrots.

SPECIAL HINTS

To fashion bread treasure chest (see photo insert), slice off the top of any pullman loaf. Hollow out the bottom portion, leaving a 1-inch border. Fill with tea sandwiches. To assemble the "chest" cover, prop the remaining bread slice on two bamboo skewers threaded with olives. One at each end. Surround the treasure chest with additional sandwiches and fresh greenery or ribbon if desired.

Crunchy Egg Pinwheels
Yields 36 pinwheels.

Pinwheel sandwiches are edible spirals of color and taste. Filled and chilled, they charm the eye as well as the taste buds. Pinwheels yield a crowd-pleasing taste while remaining one of the simplest tea sandwiches to prepare. Best of all, they can be made ahead of time and frozen until the day of use.

INGREDIENTS

½ cup butter, softened
2 tablespoons chopped anchovies
1 recipe Egg Salad, page 162
½ cup chopped walnuts
3 pullman slices egg or white bread, cut
    ½ inch thick

Base: Egg or white bread
Butter: A combination of chopped anchovies and butter
Spread: Egg salad and chopped walnuts

INSTRUCTIONS

1. Combine butter and anchovies. Blend well and set aside.
2. Combine egg salad and walnuts.
3. Trim the crusts from the bread. Flatten slightly with a rolling pin.
4. Spread a thin layer of the anchovy butter evenly on the bread.
5. Spread 1 cup of the egg salad-walnut combination on the bread. Cut the bread slices in half crosswise.
6. Roll the bread gently, jelly-roll fashion fashion.
7. Wrap the rolls in foil and refrigerate for a minimum of 2 hours.
8. Cut the rolls into ½-inch-wide slices. Each roll yields 6 pinwheels.
9. Arrange on a platter and refrigerate until serving time.

Bacon-Cream Cheese Pinwheels

Yields 36 pinwheels.

INGREDIENTS

½ cup butter, softened

¼ cup barbecue sauce

8 ounces cream cheese, softened

½ cup finely chopped cooked bacon (about 8 to 10 strips)

3 pullman slices egg or white bread, cut ½ inch thick

Base: Egg or white bread

Butter: A combination of butter and barbecue sauce

Spread: Softened cream cheese and chopped bacon

INSTRUCTIONS

1. Combine softened butter with barbecue sauce and whip in a blender. Set aside.
2. Blend thoroughly cream cheese and bacon.
3. Trim the crusts from the bread. Flatten slightly with a rolling pin. Spread a thin, even layer of the butter mixture on the bread slices. Next spread approximately 1 cup of the cream cheese-bacon mixture on the bread. Cut the bread slices in half crosswise.
4. Roll the bread gently, jelly-roll fashion. Wrap the rolls in foil and freeze for a minimum of 2 hours.
5. Cut the rolls into ½-inch-wide slices.
6. Thaw, arrange on a platter and serve chilled.

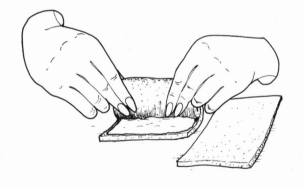

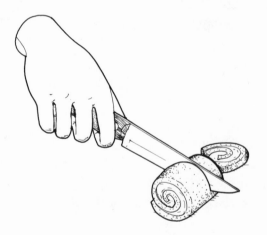

Hawaiian Chicken Triangles

Yields 32 triangles.

This hors d'oeuvre begins as large, round sandwiches and is transformed into tropical triangles. Filled with a savory blend of tempting flavors, Hawaiian triangles combine pineapple, chicken and crunchy walnuts, accented with ginger and a hint of mint.

INGREDIENTS

½ cup butter, softened

2 tablespoons crushed candied ginger

1 cup chopped cooked chicken

½ cup crushed pineapple, well drained

¼ cup chopped walnuts

1 tablespoon mayonnaise-style salad dressing

4 pullman slices egg or white bread cut ½ inch thick, or 8 4X4 sandwich slices

4 ounces cream cheese, softened

½ cup chopped mint*

½ teaspoon turmeric

SPECIAL EQUIPMENT

Pastry bag with star tip

4-inch round cookie cutter (a handy substitute is a 1-pound coffee can)

Base: Egg or white bread

Butter: A combination of softened butter and ground ginger

Spread: A combination of chicken, crushed pineapple, chopped walnuts and mayonnaise-style salad dressing

Garnish: Star made of turmeric-tinted cream cheese and finely chopped mint

*If fresh mint is unavailable, fresh chopped parsley may be substituted.

INSTRUCTIONS

1. Combine the butter with the candied ginger and blend thoroughly. Set aside.

2. Combine chicken, pineapple, walnuts and salad dressing. Blend thoroughly and set aside.

3. Cut the bread into 8 4-inch rounds with the cookie cutter. Spread each round with a thin layer of ginger butter, reserving enough for garnish.

4. Spread an even layer of the chicken mixture on four rounds and cover with the remaining 4 rounds to make 4 sandwiches.

5. Cut the rounds into 8 equal triangles. Spread the rounded edges of the triangles with the remaining ginger butter and dip in the chopped mint.

6. To garnish each triangle, combine cream cheese with turmeric. Blend well and place into a star-tipped pastry bag. Pipe a yellow star in the center of each triangle.

7. Arrange on a platter and refrigerate until serving time.

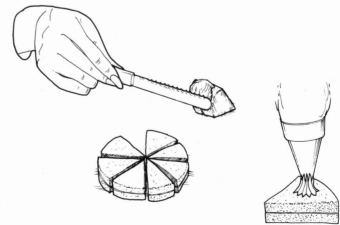

Tea Rolls

The tea roll is a long, dainty version of the pinwheel. The colorful contrast of fresh green parsley and tomato-red egg yolk add spice to the taste and color of your platter. They're easy, too—just roll and refrigerate.

INGREDIENTS
½ cup butter, softened
½ teaspoon celery seed
1 recipe Tuna Salad, page 162
30 4X4 sandwich slices egg or white
  bread
½ cup chopped parsley
4 hard-cooked egg yolks
1 tablespoon tomato paste

SPECIAL EQUIPMENT
Pastry bag with star tip

Base: Egg or white bread
Butter: Butter combined with celery seed
Spread: Tuna salad combined with pickle relish
Garnish: Tomato paste combined with egg yolks, formed into a flower with a star-tipped pastry bag, and finely chopped parsley

INSTRUCTIONS
1. Combine butter with celery seed. Blend thoroughly. Set aside.
2. Whip tuna salad in a blender or food processor until smooth.
3. Flatten the bread slices slightly with a rolling pin. Spread them with a thin layer of the seasoned butter. Next add a layer of the tuna mixture.
4. Trim the crusts and roll the bread into a tight roll.
5. Butter the ends of the rolls and dip each into the parsley. Shake off any excess.

6. In a mixing bowl, combine egg yolks and tomato paste. Fill a star-tipped pastry bag with the mixture and pipe a small star flower onto each bread roll.
7. Arrange on a platter and refrigerate until serving time.

SPECIAL HINTS
These rolls may be made the day before serving them. Store them in the freezer ungarnished. Apply the garnish just before serving.

Orange-Ginger Crescents

Fun to make, pretty to look at and, of course, delightful to eat, these sweet but tangy finger sandwiches are the perfect answer for an afternoon gathering. The touch of candied ginger adds a mysterious, sweet taste that will please any hors d'oeuvre connoisseur.

INGREDIENTS

1 cup unsalted butter, softened
3 tablespoons grated orange peel
¼ cup finely chopped candied ginger
16 ounces cream cheese, softened
3 cans (11 ounces each) tangerines
  (mandarin oranges)
10 pullman slices white or egg bread,
  cut ¼ inch thick, or 30 4X4
  sandwich slices

SPECIAL EQUIPMENT
Crescent-shaped cookie cutter

Base: Egg or white bread
Butter: A blend of softened sweet butter mixed with grated orange peel
Spread: Softened cream cheese blended with candied ginger and chopped tangerines
Garnish: Cream cheese and tangerine sections

INSTRUCTIONS

1. Combine butter and grated orange peel and blend thoroughly. Set aside.
2. Chop the ginger in a blender or food processor. Thoroughly blend with the cream cheese. Reserving 1 can of whole sections, cut the remaining tangerine sections into tiny pieces and drain them on absorbent paper. Combine with the candied ginger and cream cheese and mix thoroughly.
3. Spread a thin layer of the orange butter on all the bread slices.
4. Next spread an even layer of the cream cheese mixture on half of the bread slices. Top with the remaining bread to form a sandwich.
5. With a sharp cookie cutter, gently punch out crescent-shaped sandwiches. This process is easy because the bread is so thin.
6. Apply a small dab of softened cream cheese to the top of each crescent and top the cream cheese with a whole drained tangerine section.
7. Arrange on a platter and refrigerate until serving time.

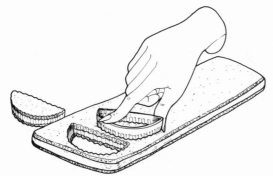

Stuffed Baguette

A cousin to the French roll, the baguette is longer and thinner, with a slightly softer crust. It can be stuffed with a hearty spread, sliced and served—adding a decorative French country flair to your buffet. Preparation time is short; the taste, magnifique!

INGREDIENTS

½ cup butter, softened
1 whole pimiento, well drained
1 recipe Turkey Salad, page 161
2 tablespoons Worcestershire sauce
1 French baguette
2-ounce jar pimiento-stuffed olives

Base: French baguette, approximately 18 inches long, most commonly found in a French bakery or delicatessen
Butter: Butter whipped with a canned whole pimiento
Spread: Turkey salad seasoned with Worcestershire sauce
Garnish: Pimiento-stuffed green olives

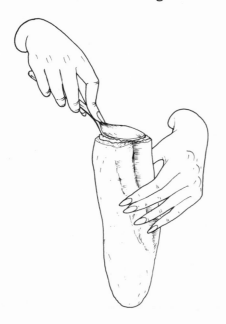

INSTRUCTIONS

1. Combine softened butter with pimiento. Whip in a blender until thoroughly combined. The butter will appear pink with small flecks of red pimiento.
2. Combine the turkey salad with Worcestershire sauce and whip in a blender until smooth.
3. Cut the baguette in thirds so you have three 6-inch loaves. Hollow out the insides of the three loaves, leaving a thin bread border.

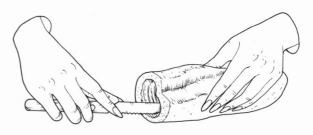

4. Spread the hollows of the baguettes all the way around with the pimiento butter.
5. Fill the loaves with the turkey spread, gently pressing the spread down to avoid air pockets. Fill the entire length of the loaves.
6. Wrap the stuffed baguettes in foil and refrigerate for several hours to set.
7. Before serving time, slice the baguettes into ½-inch rounds. Use an extra-sharp knife for clean, straight edges.
8. Slice the olives and center a slice on each baguette round.
9. Arrange on a platter and refrigerate until serving time.

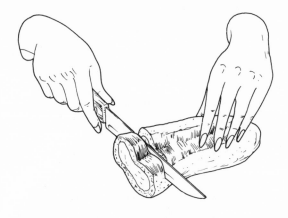

SPECIAL HINTS
Baguettes may be prepared the morning they are to be served. Wrap in foil and refrigerate ungarnished. Slice and garnish just before serving.

Rainbow Sandwiches

Yields will vary according to cutting design used.

These sandwiches offer a fast, foolproof way to add panache to your table. As their name implies, they create a rainbow of colors, textures and tastes. Results are always magnificent!

INGREDIENTS

2 pullman loaves—1 white, 1 dark—cut horizontally into ¼-inch slices
¾ cup butter, softened
1 recipe Ham Salad, page 162
1 recipe Egg Salad, page 162

Base: White and dark bread
Butter: Softened butter
Spreads: Egg salad and ham salad

INSTRUCTIONS

1. Place 2 pullman slices white bread and 1 slice dark bread on a cutting board. Lightly butter the breads.
2. Generously spread the ham mixture on one pullman slice. Cover with the dark bread, buttered side down, sandwich-style.
3. Butter the dark bread slice and spread it with a layer of egg salad. Cover with the white bread. You now have alternating layers of breads and spreads.
4. Do not trim the crusts. Wrap the entire pullman sandwich in foil and place in the freezer for one hour to set filling.
5. Remove from freezer, trim the crusts from bread and cut into any of the patterns on page 31. My favorites are numbers 1, 2 and 4.
6. Arrange the sandwiches on a platter and refrigerate until serving time.

Date-Nut Sandwiches

Yields 30 to 35 sandwiches.

These date-nut tea sandwiches are a delicate combination of sweet and meat. The refreshing taste is appropriate for the most elegant of afternoon affairs.

INGREDIENTS

1 cup chopped cooked ham

5 ounces cream cheese

½ cup crushed pineapple, well drained

2 tablespoons chopped maraschino
cherries

¾ cup butter, softened

30 slices date-nut bread, chilled and
cut into ½-inch slices or 20 4X4
sandwich slices date-nut bread

SPECIAL EQUIPMENT

Pastry bag with star tip

Base: Date-nut bread

Spread: Combination of ham, cream cheese, pineapple and maraschino cherries

Garnish: Cream cheese

INSTRUCTIONS

1. In a mixing bowl, combine the ham, 4 ounces of the cream cheese, the pineapple and maraschino cherries. Blend thoroughly.
2. Spread a thin layer of butter on the date-nut bread.
3. Spread the filling on the bread and top with another bread slice.
4. Cut the bread into shapes. If square slices are used, I suggest you choose from cuts #9, 10, 11, 12 or 14. Try cut #17 if round loaves are used, or, if they're small enough already, leave them as they are.
5. To garnish, fill a star-tipped pastry bag with the remaining cream cheese and pipe a cream cheese flower in the center of each date-nut sandwich.
6. Arrange on a platter and refrigerate until serving time.

Watercress-Olive Tea Sandwiches

Yields from 27 larger sandwiches to 96 tiny sandwiches, depending upon the cutting design used.

What tea would be complete without watercress sandwiches. Dainty, delicate and refreshing. Best of all, they're easy to prepare and fast to assemble.

INGREDIENTS

16 ounces cream cheese, softened

¾ cup finely chopped watercress
(about 2 bunches)

¼ cup finely chopped pimiento-stuffed
olives (2-ounce jar)

INSTRUCTIONS:

1. Combine cream cheese, watercress and olives. Blend thoroughly.
2. Spread a thin layer of whipped butter on the bread slices.
3. Spread a generous layer of the cream cheese

¾ cup butter, softened and whipped until fluffy

6 pullman slices egg or white bread, cut ½ inch thick, or 18 4X4 sandwich slices.

Base: Egg or white bread
Butter: Whipped butter
Spread: A combination of cream cheese, watercress and chopped olives

mixture on half of the buttered bread slices used. Cover with the remaining slices, sandwich-style.

4. Wrap the sandwiches in foil and refrigerate a minimum of 2 hours.

5. Trim the crusts and cut into bread design #1 through #6 for long pullman slices or into designs #8 through #17 for 4X4 slices.

6. Arrange on a platter and refrigerate until serving time. Serve chilled.

BREAD CUTTING PATTERNS

Pullman Slices

1 — Yields 13 slices

2 — Yields 12 slices

3 — Yields 20 slices

4 — Yields 16 slices

5 — Yields 8 rounds

6 — Yields 32 slices

7 — Yields 9 slices

4X4 Bread Slices

8 — Yields 3 slices

9 — Yields 3 slices

10 — Yields 3 slices

11 — Yields 4 slices

12 — Yields 4 slices

13 — Yields 4 slices

14 — Yields 4 slices

15 — Yields 4 slices

16 — Yields 4 slices

17 — Yields 2 slices

18 — Yields 4 slices

19 — Yields 4 slices

Three

❧ Smørrebrøds
(Open-Faced Scandinavian Sandwiches)

❧ Smørrebrød, which means buttered bread, is a Scandinavian creation that lends itself as easily to hors d'oeuvre trays as to luncheon plates. Assembled on a hearty, heavy bread, such as sour rye or dark pumpernickel, these open-faced sandwiches feature old-world delicacies, imported fish, meats and cheeses, as well as fresh vegetables. These sandwiches are typically more substantial than traditional canapés or tea sandwiches. They can provide an abundant buffet, or, as snacks, make delightful finger food. Two or three different varieties of smørrebrød could cleverly be served as an impromptu meal to be eaten with knife and fork.

These sandwiches are so artfully folded, overlapped and stacked that they far surpass their original simple description. No two look exactly alike. The multitude of colors and designs possible give your artistic hand total creative freedom as you craft individual collages of textures and taste.

Smørrebrøds are extremely versatile. While each recipe is designed to yield 30 sandwiches, you can easily adjust individual recipes to suit your particular purpose. Increase the size of the recipe, vary the size of the bread base and watch the gallery of sandwiches expand into an exciting smorgasbord!

For best results, these mini-deli sandwiches should be prepared on the day they'll be served. Allow several hours for refrigeration, since chilling enhances the flavors of these exotic spreads and adds that final flourish to make your Scandinavian smørrebrøds firm, fresh and fabulous.

DO-AHEAD NOTE
Prepare your smørrebrøds several hours before serving time. Arrange them attractively on a serving tray and cover with refrigerator paper. At party time, just remove the wrapping and serve.

Caviar-Egg Smørrebrøds

Yields 30 sandwiches.

INGREDIENTS

½ cup butter, softened
2 tablespoons grated lemon peel
1 teaspoon fresh lemon juice
8 hard-cooked eggs
¾ cup finely chopped chives
6-ounce jar black caviar
2 small lemons
30 slices egg or dark bread

SPECIAL EQUIPMENT
Small mesh strainer
Zester (optional)

Base: Thin, firm dark bread
Butter: A blend of whipped butter and grated lemon peel, sparked with a squeeze of fresh lemon juice
Spread: Black caviar, hard-cooked egg yolk which has been forced through a strainer, chopped egg white and minced fresh chives
Garnish: Lemon slices

INSTRUCTIONS

1. Combine butter, lemon peel and lemon juice. Whip in a blender or by hand.
2. Generously butter the bread slices with the lemon butter and cut them into 2½X3½-inch rectangles.
3. Peel the hard-cooked eggs while still warm to prevent discoloration. Remove the yolks and force them through a strainer into a bowl.
4. Finely chop the egg whites.
5. Mentally divide the rectangles into four equal strips. With a spoon, sprinkle the strained egg yolk on the first strip and chives on the second; spread caviar on the third and sprinkle chopped egg white on the fourth, making sure the bread is completely covered. (You may vary the order, but I've found this to be the tastiest and most attractive.)
6. Slice the lemons and cut each slice into fourths. Place the tiny lemon triangles on 2 opposite corners of each smørrebrød.
7. Refrigerate until serving time.

SPECIAL HINTS

Use the smallest lemons available for garnishing. For an especially decorative touch, cut the lemon peel with a zester (see Garnishes, page 164).

Roast Beef Smørrebrøds

Yields 30 sandwiches.

INGREDIENTS

½ cup mayonnaise
½ cup thick steak sauce
1 pound sliced roast beef
1 pound Cheddar cheese, sliced
30 slices corn flour or rye bread
2 firm small tomatoes
1 small cucumber

Base: Corn flour or rye bread
Butter: Mayonnaise and steak sauce
Spread: Roast beef strips and Cheddar cheese strips
Garnish: Tomato-cucumber twist

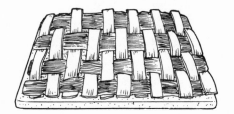

INSTRUCTIONS

1. Combine the mayonnaise and steak sauce and mix well. Refrigerate until time for use.
2. Cut the roast beef slices into ½-inch-wide strips approximately 5 inches long.
3. Slice the Cheddar cheese into ½-inch-wide strips approximately 4 inches long.
4. Spread the bread slices with the mayonnaise mixture.
5. Cut the bread into 2½X3½-inch rectangles.
6. Place 4 roast beef strips side by side lengthwise on each piece of bread.
7. Weave 6 strips of cheese over and under the roast beef in a basketweave pattern.
8. Trim off the excess. (Save the trimmings for salads!)
9. To garnish this woven work of art, nothing but the freshest of vegetables will do. Slice a firm tomato and scored cucumber.
10. Place about ½ teaspoon of the mayonnaise-steak sauce mixture on the center of the woven roast beef and cheese. Top with the tomato and cucumber making a simultaneous twist (see Garnishes, page 164).
11. Refrigerate until serving time.

SPECIAL HINTS

The roast beef and Cheddar cheese should be sliced thin to medium for best results.

Prosciutto-Cantaloupe Smørrebrøds

Yields 30 sandwiches.

INGREDIENTS

16 ounces cream cheese, softened
½ cup finely chopped fresh mint or parsley
1 small cantaloupe
30 slices black raisin bread
½ pound prosciutto ham

Base: Black raisin bread
Butter: A combination of freshly chopped mint and cream cheese
Spread: Cantaloupe wrapped in prosciutto
Garnish: Cantaloupe twist

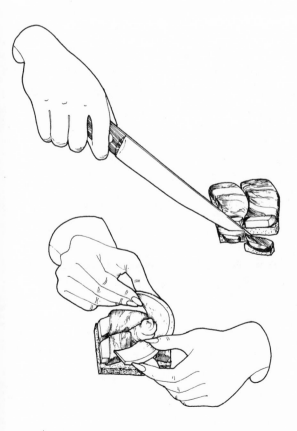

INSTRUCTIONS

1. Combine the chopped mint with the cream cheese. Mix thoroughly and allow to stand at room temperature.
2. Cut the cantaloupe into quarters. Remove the peel and discard the seeds. Slice thinly.
3. Spread the mint cream cheese generously on the raisin bread. Cut the bread into 3X3-inch squares.
4. Wrap the prosciutto slices delicately around the cantaloupe slices until they are completely covered.
5. Place the wrapped melon slices side by side on the buttered bread until no bread is visible. Trim the extra melon from the sides of the bread. (Leftovers may be used in a salad, so do save them.)
6. Place a dab of the mint cream cheese mixture on top of the row of wrapped melon.
7. For the garnish, cut a thin sliver of cantaloupe and create a cantaloupe twist by turning the ends in opposite directions (see Garnishes, page 165). The cream cheese will hold the twist in shape.
8. Refrigerate until serving time.

SPECIAL HINTS

Paper-thin slices of prosciutto, the delicious Italian ham, make a perfect wrapping for the cantaloupe. However, if prosciutto is not available, substitute thin slices of your favorite brand of ham.

Cold Cut Smørrebrøds

INGREDIENTS

½ cup butter, softened
1 small head escarole or lettuce
60 slices Cheddar cheese
60 slices bologna
30 slices rye bread
6 to 8 tomatoes, thinly sliced to yield 60 slices
60 salami slices

SPECIAL EQUIPMENT

4-inch round cutter
3-inch round cutter

Base: Rye bread
Butter: Whipped butter
Spread: Escarole, salami, Cheddar cheese and bologna
Garnish: Salami rosette

INSTRUCTIONS

1. Whip butter and allow to stand at room temperature.
2. Rinse, dry and refrigerate the escarole.
3. Cut the cheese and bologna into rounds with the 3-inch cutter.
4. Cut the rye bread into rounds with the 4-inch cutter.
5. Generously butter the bread with the whipped butter.
6. Tear a small handful of the escarole and cover the bread with the fluffy greenery.
7. Overlap the rounds of tomato, cheese and meats on top of the escarole in a circular design beginning with the tomato slices then bologna, then cheese and finally salami. Repeat the sequence. Eight slices colorfully complete this tasty wheel.
8. Apply a dab of soft whipped butter to the center of the circles. Fashion a small salami rose (see Garnishes, page 165) and place in the center of the butter, which, when chilled, will secure the shape of this unusual rose.
9. Refrigerate until serving time.

SPECIAL HINTS

Purchase a good, firm salami, approximately 3 inches in diameter.
The slices of tomato, cheese and cold cuts will extend beyond the bread to form a bountiful sandwich. Serve these sandwiches on plates.

Alpine Smørrebrøds

Yields 30 sandwiches.

INGREDIENTS

3½-ounce can of skinless and boneless
  sardines, very well drained
½ cup butter, softened
30 slices black raisin bread
¾ pound Swiss cheese, thinly sliced
1 pint cherry tomatoes
2 fresh green peppers

Base: Sliced black raisin bread
Butter: Mixture of sardines and butter
Spread: Rolled Swiss cheese
Garnish: Cherry tomatoes and
chopped green peppers

INSTRUCTIONS

1. Prepare the sardine butter by mixing the well-drained sardines and the softened butter. This may be done in a blender or by hand. Set mixture aside at room temperature.
2. Cut the bread slices and Swiss cheese into 3½X2½-inch rectangles.
3. Slice the cherry tomatoes and finely chop the green pepper.
4. Spread the sardine butter generously on the bread rectangles. Loosely roll 3 of the cut Swiss cheese rectangles so that they will lie slightly flattened on the bread. Place them next to each other on the bread. Flatten the cheese rolls on the bread by gently pressing with the flat side of a knife blade. The top of the bread should be completely covered.
5. Tuck the sliced cherry tomatoes in a line between each cheese roll.
6. Sprinkle the chopped green pepper in a line down the length of the entire smørrebrød on top of the cheese and tomatoes.
7. Refrigerate until serving time.

SPECIAL HINTS

Since sardines are soft in texture they need not be chopped prior to mixing with the whipped butter. A little blending will achieve a smooth consistency.
A good, thinly sliced Swiss cheese will make this smørrebrød outstanding. I usually choose an imported Swiss, as the imports have a distinctive flavor.
Raisin bread adds a contrasting sweet taste to the sandwich. If it is not available, a heavy black bread would be a delicious substitute.

Smoked Oyster Smørrebrøds

Yields 30 sandwiches.

INGREDIENTS

6 hard-cooked eggs
16 ounces cream cheese, softened
½ teaspoon dried dill
3 cans (3½ ounces each) smoked oysters
30 slices whole wheat bread
30 cherry tomatoes

SPECIAL EQUIPMENT

Egg slicer

Base: Wheat bread
Butter: Combination of softened cream cheese and dill
Spread: Smoked oysters and sliced hard-cooked eggs
Garnish: Cherry tomato rosettes

INSTRUCTIONS

1. Peel the hard-cooked eggs while still warm to prevent discoloration and slice with an egg slicer.
2. Prepare the butter by combining cream cheese with dill. Mix and set aside at room temperature.
3. Drain and chop the smoked oysters.
4. Cut the bread into 3X3-inch squares.
5. Fashion the tomato rosettes (see Garnishes, page 165) and refrigerate.
6. Generously spread the dilled cream cheese on the bread, reserving about 1 teaspoon for garnish.
7. Spread the chopped oysters to all corners of the bread.
8. Overlap egg slices in a diagonal line dividing the bread into two triangles.
9. Apply a dab of dilled cream cheese to the center of one triangle on each slice and top with a tomato rosette.
10. Refrigerate until serving time.

SPECIAL HINTS

If it's available, fresh dill adds an authentic touch of old-world flavor.
Be sure to drain the oysters thoroughly.

Avocado-Turkey Smørrebrøds

Yields 30 sandwiches.

INGREDIENTS

½ cup butter, softened and whipped

2 large garlic cloves, peeled and
crushed

½ cup mayonnaise

½ cup prepared mustard

30 slices shepherd's bread or white
bread

1 ½ pounds prepared rolled smoked
turkey, thinly sliced

5 medium-size firm, ripe avocados

Base: Sliced shepherd's bread
Butter: Garlic butter, a combination of
fresh garlic and whipped butter
Spread: Thinly sliced smoked turkey
Garnish: Ripe avocado slices topped
with mustard-mayonnaise sauce

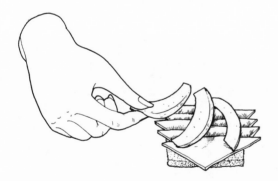

INSTRUCTIONS

1. Prepare the garlic butter by combining whipped butter with freshly crushed garlic cloves. Crush the cloves in a garlic press or with the flat side of a wide-bladed knife. Set the mixture aside at room temperature.

2. Combine the mayonnaise and mustard. Mix well, then refrigerate.

3. Cut the bread into 3X3-inch squares and spread with the garlic butter.

4. Cut the turkey slices into 3X3-inch squares and then in half so you have 2 triangles approximately half the size of the bread squares. Place 4 turkey triangles on the bread all pointing in the same direction. They will overlap and entirely cover the bread.

5. Peel and cut each avocado into ninths.

6. Place 3 slices of avocado on the turkey triangles in a fanlike pattern.

7. Spoon the chilled mustard mayonnaise with a generous hand neatly across the fanned avocado slices.

8. Refrigerate until serving time.

SPECIAL HINTS

Rolled smoked turkey, the primary ingredient, should be chosen with care. I prefer to have it freshly cut to order at the deli, but it can be purchased prepackaged. Either way, do be sure it is thinly sliced.

Liverwurst Smørrebrøds

INGREDIENTS

1 small head escarole
30 slices rye bread
1 cup mayonnaise-style salad dressing
1 pound liverwurst
1 pint cherry tomatoes
16-ounce jar pitted black or green olives
2 cucumbers

SPECIAL EQUIPMENT
Zester

Base: Rye bread
Butter: Mayonnaise-style salad dressing
Spread: Liverwurst
Garnish: Sliced cherry tomatoes, cucumbers, olives and escarole

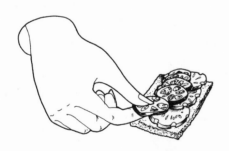

INSTRUCTIONS

1. Rinse the escarole. Tear a handful into small shreds. Place on moist paper towels and refrigerate.
2. Cut the rye bread into 2½X3½-inch rectangles.
3. Spread a thin layer of salad dressing on the rectangles.
4. Spread the liverwurst generously on top.
5. Slice the cherry tomatoes and olives. Score the cucumber peel with a zester (see Garnishes, page 164) and slice it diagonally.
6. Overlap cucumber slices along the center of the bread in a line stretching the length of the rectangle. Center the tomato slices in a line on top of the cucumber and arrange sliced olives on top of the tomatoes. Now you have 3 layers of fresh vegetables.
7. Place the chilled escarole on either side of the vegetable layers.
8. Refrigerate until serving time.

SPECIAL HINTS

I specifically suggest escarole because of its curly leaves, vibrant color and delicate texture. It's a special touch that adds visual appeal to this sandwich.

Shrimp Smørrebrøds

INGREDIENTS

16 ounces cream cheese, softened

1 envelope green goddess salad dressing mix

1 tablespoon sour cream

1 pound precooked baby shrimp

2 cans (4 ounces each) whole pimientos

8-ounce jar pimiento-stuffed green olives

30 thin slices pumpernickel bread

Base: Thinly sliced hard pumpernickel bread

Butter: A combination of green goddess salad mix, cream cheese and sour cream

Spread: Chopped baby shrimp and chopped pimiento-stuffed olives

Garnish: Whole pimiento, sliced into strips

INSTRUCTIONS

1. Combine cream cheese with green goddess salad dressing mix. Add a tablespoon of sour cream for creamy texture and whip in a blender. Set aside at room temperature.
2. Rinse, drain and coarsely chop the shrimp.
3. Thoroughly drain whole pimientos and slice into thin strips about 4½ inches long. Set aside.
4. Coarsely chop the olives.
5. Cut the bread into 3X3-inch squares and generously spread with cream cheese mixture.
6. Mentally divide the bread square in half diagonally and then in half again, forming 4 imaginary triangles.
7. Spoon the chopped shrimp onto two opposite triangles.
8. Spoon the chopped olives onto the remaining two triangles.
9. Garnish the design by placing 2 long pimiento strips in a X shape, extending from one corner of the bread diagonally to the other, clearly distinguishing the triangular pattern.
10. Refrigerate until serving time.

SPECIAL HINTS

Make sure you drain the pimientos well before slicing. To get the longest, solid strips of pimiento, use slices cut from the widest portion of the whole pimiento.

Black olives can be used if you prefer, but the piquant salty taste of the green olives adds spice to this sandwich, and the green and red confetti effect adds still another colorful dimension.

Salmon Smørrebrøds

Yields 30 sandwiches.

INGREDIENTS

16 ounces cream cheese, softened
2 tablespoons grated lemon peel
4 small white boiling onions
½ cup butter, softened
30 slices egg bread, prepared as croustades, see page 110
1½ pounds smoked salmon, thinly sliced
Fresh mint or parsley

SPECIAL EQUIPMENT
Pastry bag with shell tip

Base: Egg bread croustade
Butter: Whipped butter
Spread: Thin slices of smoked salmon wrapped around cream cheese and grated lemon peel mixture.
Garnish: Small boiling onions and a sprig of fresh mint or parsley

INSTRUCTIONS

1. Prepare the filling for the salmon rolls by combining cream cheese with grated lemon peel. Set aside at room temperature.
2. Thinly slice peeled boiling onions and separate the rings.
3. Generously butter the egg bread croustades and cut into 2½X3½-inch rectangles.
4. Place one teaspoon of the cream cheese mixture at one long end of the sliced salmon, and roll up the slice.
5. Using a sharp knife, cut the salmon rolls in 2½-inch pieces, so they'll fit neatly on the bread.
6. Place 3 or 4 salmon rolls side by side on the buttered bread.
7. Fill a shell-tipped pastry bag with the remaining cream cheese and pipe shells across the center of the salmon rolls.
8. Overlap 5 to 8 onion rings on top of the cream cheese shells.
9. Top with a fresh sprig of mint or parsley and refrigerate until serving time.

SPECIAL HINTS

I suggest using freshly sliced smoked salmon rather than the prepackaged kind since there is a considerable taste difference.
Make the salmon rolls as uniform in size as possible for optimum eye appeal.

Danish Ham Smørrebrøds

INGREDIENTS

½ cup sweet butter, softened
1 cup chopped gherkins
1 bunch radishes
60 thin slices Monterey Jack cheese
60 thin slices Danish ham
30 slices thick-textured pumpernickel
    bread
½ cup mayonnaise

Base: Thick-textured black bread
Butter: Whipped sweet butter
Spread: Alternating folded slices of
ham and cheese
Garnish: Finely chopped gherkins and
thinly sliced radishes

INSTRUCTIONS

1. Whip butter and set aside at room temperature.
2. Finely chop gherkins and thinly slice the radishes.
3. Cut the cheese and ham into 2½X3½-inch rectangles and loosely fold over. Set aside.
4. Generously butter the black bread and cut into 2½X3½-inch rectangles.
5. Alternate the folded cheese and ham slices, overlapping them on the bread.
6. Sprinkle the chopped gherkins between the ham and cheese folds.
7. Spoon a thin line of mayonnaise lengthwise across the folded ham and cheese.
8. Overlap radish slices on top of the mayonnaise.
9. Refrigerate until serving time.

SPECIAL HINTS

About 4 alternating slices of ham and cheese folds will fit each slice of bread.
Trim the ends of the ham and cheese rolls for a clean, finished look.

Four

❧ Barquettes

❧ Barquettes offer a wonderful opportunity to exercise your culinary creativity. Each one becomes an expression of yourself, your own tiny work of art. Fashioned from pastry into delicate boat shapes with fluted edges, they serve as elegant containers for a delightful array of fillings. You can decorate them with garnishes, such as olives and pimientos cut into all sorts of shapes and sizes, and arrange them in dramatic color combinations to create a very appealing hors d'oeuvre tray.

Even if you've never attempted barquettes before, they're so simple to make you'll find yourself quickly becoming an expert. Just prepare the barquette shells as directed, select the fillings and garnishes of your choice and allow your imagination full rein. Very tasty and easy to prepare, they provide a decorative canvas for a scrumptious palette of ingredients. Depending on the way you serve them and the garnishes you choose, you can make them as elegant or as informal as you wish.

DO-AHEAD NOTE

You can prepare the barquette shells without the fillings up to two weeks in advance and freeze them, or purchase them ready-made from your bakery.

Prepare the fillings a day ahead of time and refrigerate them until needed. Cut the garnishes just before assembling your creations to assure freshness. Then chill and serve.

SPECIAL HINTS

Spread the fillings on the barquettes very gently so that you have a smooth surface on which to apply the garnishes. The fillings spread easiest when they are at room temperature, so remove them from the refrigerator and allow them to stand for a while before spreading them on the barquettes.

Barquette Pastry Shells

These infinitely versatile pastry boats are waiting to be filled with a variety of smooth, tasty spreads. They're flaky, yet sturdy and deliciously edible.

INGREDIENTS

2⅔ cups flour
½ teaspoon salt
½ cup shortening
6 to 8 tablespoons cold water

SPECIAL EQUIPMENT

Barquette molds
Dried beans

INSTRUCTIONS

1. Preheat the oven to 475 degrees. In a mixing bowl, combine flour and salt. Add shortening and cut into flour using a fork or pastry blender.
2. Add water, one tablespoon at a time. Mix again until the dough sticks together and leaves the sides of the bowl. Divide the dough in half.
3. Roll out each portion of the dough to ¼-inch thickness.
4. Invert the barquette molds onto the pastry, and cut out the pastry, leaving approximately ½ inch around each mold.
5. Pat the dough into the mold, trimming the edges with your fingers at the same time.
6. Prick the edges of the molds with a fork, fill with beans for weight and arrange them on a cookie sheet.
7. Bake 8 to 10 minutes.
8. Cool completely. Remove the pastry boats from their molds.

DO-AHEAD NOTE

Barquette shells may be made in advance and stored in a moisture-proof container or frozen until the day you need them.

Ham Barquettes

Yields 30 barquettes.

Impress your guests with your culinary artistry! Working with the delicate color combinations of ham, asparagus and pimiento, you can create a barquette masterpiece.

INGREDIENTS

1½ cups ground cooked ham
1 tablespoon mayonnaise-style salad
  dressing
Garlic powder to taste
Dash of ground cloves
Cooked asparagus spears or scallions
Whole pimiento
30 prebaked Barquette Pastry Shells,
  page 45

Base: Barquette shells
Filling: Ham and mayonnaise salad dressing
Garnish: Asparagus spears and pimiento

INSTRUCTIONS

1. In a blender combine ham, salad dressing, garlic powder and cloves. Blend until smooth.
2. Slice the asparagus spears or scallions into thin slivers the length of the barquette. Cut tiny circles out of the pimiento.
3. Spread the ham filling on each barquette, leaving a smooth surface.
4. To garnish, lay one asparagus or scallion sliver on top of each barquette. Accent with 3 pimiento dots.
5. Refrigerate and serve chilled.

Liver Paté and Truffles Barquettes

Yields 30 barquettes.

Oh, the precious truffles! Nature's gift from the soil. Use them as a garnish for that gourmet delight, liver paté, and you have a barquette extraordinaire!

INGREDIENTS

12 ounces (1½ cups), liver paté
30 prebaked Barquette Pastry Shells,
  page 45
1-ounce can truffles

Base: Barquette shells
Filling: Liver paté
Garnish: Truffles

SPECIAL EQUIPMENT
Aspic cutters

INSTRUCTIONS

1. Spread the paté on each barquette shell, leaving a smooth surface.
2. Using aspic cutters, cut truffles into tiny shapes. Align them down the center of the barquettes.
3. Refrigerate and serve chilled.

Sardine-Egg Barquettes

Yields 30 barquettes.

A refreshing blend of sardines, cream cheese and scallions makes for tasty barquettes that are colorfully ornamented with slices of eggs and pimiento rounds.

INGREDIENTS

2 cans (3¾ ounces each) skinless and boneless sardines
4 ounces cream cheese, softened
1 tablespoon minced scallion
½ teaspoon dill
2 hard-cooked eggs
4-ounce jar whole pimientos
30 prebaked Barquette Pastry Shells, page 45

SPECIAL EQUIPMENT
Aspic cutters
Egg slicer

Base: Barquette shells
Filling: Sardines, cream cheese, scallion
Garnish: sliced eggs, pimiento

INSTRUCTIONS

1. Combine sardines, cream cheese, scallion and dill in a blender.
2. Spread the sardine filling on each barquette shell, leaving a smooth surface.
3. Slice the hard-cooked eggs with the egg slicer for uniform slices. With a round, ripple-edged aspic cutter, cut tiny rounds out of the whole pimiento. With a smaller, smooth-edged aspic cutter, remove the centers from the rounds so they resemble tiny donuts.
4. Center an egg slice on each barquette. Place the pimiento rounds on top of the egg. Dot each barquette tip with pimiento.
5. Refrigerate and serve chilled.

Cheese-Bacon Barquettes

Yields 30 barquettes.

These crunchy cheese and bacon delights bloom with flavor and a lovely cocktail onion and pimiento "flower."

INGREDIENTS

1 cup spreadable Cheddar cheese, softened
2 ounces cream cheese, softened
¼ cup cooked, crumbled bacon (about 3 strips)
1 teaspoon Worcestershire sauce
30 prebaked Barquette Pastry Shells, page 45
4-ounce jar cocktail onions
Pimiento slices

Base: Barquette shells
Filling: Cheese and bacon
Garnish: Cocktail onions and pimiento

INSTRUCTIONS

1. In a blender, combine Cheddar cheese, cream cheese, bacon and Worcestershire sauce. Blend thoroughly.
2. Spread the cheese-bacon mixture on each barquette shell, leaving a smooth surface.
3. Slice the cocktail onions into thin rounds. Arrange 6 slices so they overlap in a circular pattern resembling a flower in the center of each barquette.
4. Dot the center of the flower and 2 points of each barquette with pimiento.
5. Refrigerate and serve chilled.

Caviar Barquettes

Yields 30 barquettes.

A barquette fit for royalty. Start with a layer of cream cheese, egg and onion. Then stripe it with alternating diagonals of red and black caviar. What a lavish and colorful feast!

INGREDIENTS

3 hard-cooked eggs, chopped
1 teaspoon minced onion
4 ounces cream cheese, softened
30 prebaked Barquette Pastry Shells, page 45
3-ounce jar black caviar
3-ounce jar red caviar

INSTRUCTIONS

1. In a mixing bowl, combine the chopped eggs, minced onion and cream cheese. Blend until smooth and creamy.
2. Spread the egg mixture on the barquette shells, leaving a smooth surface.
3. Arrange the black and red caviar in diagonal strips across the barquettes.

Base: Barquette shells
Filling: Eggs, onion and cream cheese
Garnish: Black and red caviar

4. Refrigerate and serve chilled.

Shrimp Barquettes

Yields 30 barquettes.

For those who love shrimp, these barquettes are for you. They're filled with cream cheese, seasoned with green goddess salad dressing mix and topped with a row of miniature shrimp. All the ingredients are artfully nestled in a pastry base.

INGREDIENTS

12 ounces cream cheese, softened
1 tablespoon green goddess salad dressing mix
1 teaspoon mayonnaise-style salad dressing
1 tablespoon minced onion
30 prebaked Barquette Pastry Shells, page 45
½ pound cooked tiny shrimp
Garlic powder to taste
2-ounce jar pimiento strips

Base: Barquette shells
Filling: Cream cheese, green goddess salad dressing mix, onion
Garnish: Tiny shrimp and pimiento

INSTRUCTIONS

1. Combine cream cheese, green goddess mix, salad dressing and onion in a blender and process, or whip by hand.
2. Spread the cream cheese mixture on each barquette, leaving a smooth surface.
3. Place shrimp on top, close together, in a row facing in one direction.
4. Top the shrimp with a small strip of pimiento cut to the length of the barquette.
5. Refrigerate and serve chilled.

Tuna Diamond Barquettes

Yields 30 barquettes.

A culinary jewel! Ordinary tuna assumes an air of elegance and grace when served on a pastry base and decorated with olives, pimiento and capers.

INGREDIENTS

½ recipe (1 cup) Tuna Salad, page 162
2 ounces cream cheese
Garlic powder to taste
Whole pimientos
Pitted green olives
30 prebaked Barquette Pastry Shells, page 45
Capers

Base: Barquette shells
Filling: Tuna salad and cream cheese
Garnish: Pimiento, green olives and capers

SPECIAL EQUIPMENT
Diamond-shaped aspic cutter

INSTRUCTIONS

1. In a blender, combine tuna salad, cream cheese and garlic powder. Blend thoroughly for a smooth, creamy consistency.
2. Cut the whole pimientos into tiny diamonds with an aspic cutter and cut the olives into slivers.
3. Spread the tuna filling on each barquette, leaving a smooth surface.
4. Align the pimiento diamonds down the center, applying 2 olive slivers between each diamond. Accent 2 points of each barquette with a caper.
5. Refrigerate and serve chilled.

Roquefort-Anchovy Barquettes

Yields 30 barquettes.

The lively flavors of Roquefort and anchovy meld to form an elegant barquette that's easy to make. Just spread the cheese filling, slice the anchovies and garnish the barquettes with olives.

INGREDIENTS

4 ounces cream cheese, softened
4 ounces Roquefort cheese
30 prebaked Barquette Pastry Shells, page 45
3-ounce can flat anchovy fillets
2-ounce jar pimiento-stuffed olives

INSTRUCTIONS

1. Combine cream cheese and Roquefort in a mixing bowl. Blend thoroughly.
2. Spread the Roquefort-cream cheese mixture on each barquette, leaving a smooth surface.
3. Slice olives into thin rounds. Cut the anchovies in half lengthwise.

Base: Barquette shells
Filling: Roquefort and cream cheese
Garnish: Anchovies and
pimiento-stuffed olives

4. Place a small strip of anchovy down the center of each barquette and accent it with an olive slice at each end.
5. Refrigerate and serve chilled.

Tomato-Egg Barquettes

Yields 30 barquettes.

Smooth and spicy, that's the theme of these barquettes. Piquant tomato paste teams with egg yolk to form a flavorful filling, topped with a decorative cream cheese line and accented with pimiento-stuffed olives.

INGREDIENTS

6-ounce can tomato paste
6 hard-cooked egg yolks
¼ teaspoon garlic powder
2-ounce jar pimiento-stuffed olives
4 ounces cream cheese, softened
30 prebaked Barquette Pastry Shells,
   page 45

Base: Barquette shells
Spread: Tomato paste, egg yolk and garlic powder
Garnish: Cream cheese and
pimiento-stuffed olives

SPECIAL EQUIPMENT
Pastry bag with star tip

INSTRUCTIONS

1. Combine tomato paste, egg yolks and garlic powder in a blender. Whip until smooth.
2. Slice the olives into thin discs.
3. Fill a star-tipped pastry bag with the cream cheese.
4. Spread the tomato-egg filling on the barquettes, smoothing the surface.
5. With the pastry bag, pipe a decorative cream cheese line down the center of each barquette.
6. Garnish with an olive slice at the tips of the barquettes.

Liver Sausage and Sherry Barquettes

Yields 30 barquettes.

These barquettes are deceptively simple to make and, oh, so alluring! All it takes is liver sausage, sherry and olives. Watch how quickly they go.

INGREDIENTS

12 ounces liver sausage
2 tablespoons dry sherry
30 prebaked Barquette Pastry Shells, page 45
Pitted black olives
Pimiento-stuffed olives

Base: Barquette shells
Filling: Liver sausage and sherry
Garnish: Black and pimiento-stuffed olives

INSTRUCTIONS

1. In a mixing bowl, combine liver sausage with sherry. Blend thoroughly.
2. Spread the liver filling on each barquette, leaving a smooth surface.
3. Cut the black olives into slivers. Slice the pimiento-stuffed olives into thin rounds.
4. To garnish, alternate a green olive round with two black olive slivers arranged in a V shape down the entire length of each barquette.
5. Refrigerate and serve chilled.

Christmas Barquettes

Yields 30 barquettes.

This barquette brims with the holiday spirit, as tasty green spinach combines with the lively red of pimiento fashioned to resemble a Christmas tree.

INGREDIENTS

10-ounce package frozen chopped spinach, thawed and well drained
4 ounces cream cheese
¼ teaspoon garlic salt
1 teaspoon chopped chives
2 cans (4 ounces each) whole pimientos
30 prebaked Barquette Pastry Shells, page 45

Base: Barquette shells
Filling: Spinach cream cheese
Garnish: Pimientos

INSTRUCTIONS

1. In a blender, combine spinach, cream cheese, garlic salt and chopped chives.
2. Cut tiny Christmas trees the length of the barquette shells from the whole pimiento.
3. Spread the spinach mixture on each barquette, leaving a smooth surface.
4. To garnish, top with a pimiento Christmas tree.
5. Refrigerate and serve cold.

Five

❧ Roll-Em-Ups

❧ Quick and tempting, this collection of roll-em-ups features a variety of ingredients rolled and fastened with cellophane-tipped toothpicks for party fare. A unique twist to serving cold cuts, often having the bread on the inside, these roll-em-ups become reversed variations of cold cut sandwiches.

There's no limit to the combinations of meats, cheeses, fruits, fillings and breads you can use. In this chapter, I've provided recipes for my favorites. Each recipe yields 30 roll-em-ups. But do use your imagination to concoct your own variety of delectable rolls. Mix and interchange the fillings and wrappings. Let those flavorful ideas flow!

Most fillings can be prepared a day ahead, then rolled in their tasty wrappers several hours prior to serving. They'll keep fresh and crisp in the refrigerator while the flavors meld perfectly. Whether you serve your chilled roll-em-ups on an elegant platter or more casually in a country basket, your guests will find them irresistible, and you will, too; so make some extras.

DO-AHEAD NOTE

Relax at party time—have your roll-em-ups ready to serve. You can prepare the fillings the day before your party and refrigerate them. Then on the day of your soirée, roll up the hors d'oeuvres, arrange them attractively on a tray, cover with plastic wrap and chill for up to eight hours before serving time.

Salami-Olive Cones

Yields 30 cones.

Who can resist these tasty little horns of plenty? Salami cones delectably brimming with a piped-in filling of cream cheese and chopped olives.

INGREDIENTS

8 ounces cream cheese, softened
4½-ounce can pitted black or green olives, finely chopped
30 slices salami

SPECIAL EQUIPMENT

Pastry bag with star tip
Cellophane-tipped toothpicks

INSTRUCTIONS

1. Combine the softened cream cheese with the olives.
2. Separate the salami slices and roll each one into a cone, skewering it through the center with a toothpick.
3. Fill the star-tipped pastry bag with the cream cheese-olive mixture.
4. Place the tip of the bag into the center of the cone. Squeeze the bag as you slowly draw out the tip, finishing with a star design inside the cone.
5. Refrigerate until serving time.

Corned Beef Coronets

Yields 30 coronets.

What goes better with corned beef than cabbage? And when the combination is colorful and conveniently folded finger food, it makes hearty hors d'oeuvres for a hungry after-game crowd.

INGREDIENTS

½ recipe (1 cup) Coleslaw, page 161
¼ cup bread crumbs
30 thin slices corned beef
¼ cup prepared mustard

SPECIAL EQUIPMENT

Cellophane-tipped toothpicks

INSTRUCTIONS

1. Combine coleslaw and bread crumbs. Mix well.
2. Spread each corned beef slice lightly with mustard. Top with 1 teaspoon of coleslaw mixture.
3. Distribute the filling evenly, then roll the corned beef around the coleslaw into a neat coronet.
4. Skewer with a cellophane-tipped toothpick and refrigerate until serving time.

If you are using your own coleslaw recipe, make it extra thick to avoid drips. If using prepared coleslaw, drain off excess liquid before use.

For an especially colorful effect, use shredded red cabbage for your coleslaw.

Macaroni Cones

Yields 30 cones.

Whether your favorite macaroni salad recipe has been handed down through the generations or you accidently concocted your own winning blend, use it in this crunchy, cheesy roll-em-up recipe. What? No cherished macaroni salad secrets? Try mine.

INGREDIENTS

½ recipe (1 cup) Macaroni Salad, page 162
½ cup garlic-flavored croutons
30 slices American cheese

SPECIAL EQUIPMENT

Pie fluter (optional)
Cellophane-tipped toothpicks

INSTRUCTIONS

1. Combine macaroni salad and croutons.
2. Separate the cheese slices. Flute the edges with the pie fluter at this time if you wish to do so.
3. Place approximately 1 to 1½ teaspoons of macaroni-crouton filling on each slice, being careful to allow just enough so that the cheese can be easily folded. Shape the filling into a line the length of the cheese. Roll the cheese into a cone shape.
4. Fasten with a cellophone-tipped toothpick.
5. Refrigerate until serving time.

SPECIAL HINTS

For a fancy touch, try trimming the edges of the cheese with a pie fluter. This creates an interesting edge and requires very little time. Plus, it's fun!

To prepare the macaroni salad the day before, leave out the croutons. To insure a crunchy texture, add the croutons just before fashioning the cones.

Antipasto Roll-em-ups

Try surprising your guests by serving antipasto in a spicy roll-em-up. Convenient and tasty, this is a bellissima addition to any Italian feast.

INGREDIENTS

*30 short bread sticks, approximately 4
    inches long*

*60 large slices Italian salami, 4 inches in
    diameter*

*½ recipe (2 cups) Marinated Eggplant,
    page*

SPECIAL EQUIPMENT

Cellophane-tipped toothpicks

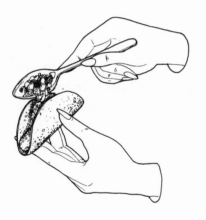

INSTRUCTIONS

1. Place a bread stick in the center of a salami slice.

2. Place a heaping teaspoonful of the marinated eggplant on top of the bread stick and spread it evenly to each end.

3. Roll the salami slice tightly around the eggplant and bread stick.

4. Roll another salami slice in the opposite direction over the first. Secure the salami by gently skewering the roll through the center catching the salami ends. The bread stick will not break if carefully skewered.

5. Refrigerate until serving time.

DO-AHEAD NOTE

To insure crisp bread sticks, prepare the antipasto roll-em-ups no more than a few hours before serving, but the marinated eggplant filling may be prepared several days in advance and refrigerated.

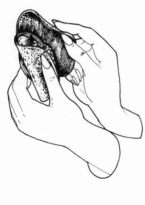

Turkey-Asparagus Roll-em-ups

Yields 30 roll-em-ups.

The elegant green asparagus teamed with a tangy yellow sauce is rolled in a pale turkey wrapper. As beautiful as they are delicious, these roll-em-ups are the perfect offering at formal or informal affairs, and they're quick and easy to prepare.

INGREDIENTS

*30 asparagus spears—fresh, frozen or
    canned*
¼ cup mayonnaise
¼ cup prepared mustard
½ cup chopped almonds
8 slices toasted white bread
30 thin slices packaged turkey

SPECIAL EQUIPMENT

Cellophane-tipped toothpicks

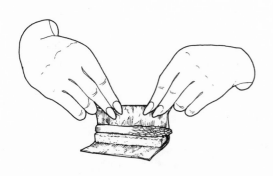

INSTRUCTIONS

1. If you use fresh or frozen asparagus spears, prepare them by steaming until just tender.
2. Cut the spears uniformly to fit the length of the turkey slices.
3. Combine the mayonnaise and mustard and mix thoroughly.
4. Trim the crusts off the toasted bread and cut each slice into 4 1-inch-wide strips. Spread the mayonnaise-mustard sauce on each toast strip. Sprinkle lightly with almonds.
5. Place an asparagus spear on the bread strip and roll up in a turkey slice.
6. Fasten the roll with a cellophane-tipped toothpick and refrigerate until serving time.

SPECIAL HINTS

Turkey slices fresh off the bird won't work in this recipe, so look for the packaged slices at the market or deli.

Trim the asparagus spears at the stalk end so that the pointed tip remains, adding a decorative effect that will extend slightly beyond the turkey slice.

Reuben Roll-em-ups

A variation on the famous Reuben sandwich, this hors d'oeuvre offers all the hearty, tasty ingredients, ingeniously rolled in a pastrami wrapper.

INGREDIENTS

4 ounces Swiss cheese, grated
1 cup sauerkraut, very well drained
¼ cup prepared mustard
30 slices pastrami

SPECIAL EQUIPMENT

Cellophane-tipped toothpicks

INSTRUCTIONS

1. Combine the Swiss cheese with the sauerkraut.
2. Spread a thin layer of mustard on each pastrami slice. Heap a generous spoonful of the cheese-sauerkraut mixture on each slice of pastrami.
3. Roll the meat tightly and skewer it through the center with a cellophane-tipped toothpick.
4. Refrigerate until serving time.

SPECIAL HINTS

For some vibrant color, dice a whole pimiento and add it to the sauerkraut mixture.

Liver Sausage-Cheese Rolls

Add a dash of sherry, and liver sausage takes on an old-world elegance. Chopped walnuts add texture and interest to these delicious roll-em-ups.

INGREDIENTS

2 ounces dry sherry
12 ounces liver sausage
½ cup chopped walnuts
30 slices Monterey Jack cheese

SPECIAL EQUIPMENT

Cellophane-tipped toothpicks

INSTRUCTIONS

1. Thoroughly mix together the sherry, liver sausage and walnuts. Refrigerate for at least 1 hour.
2. Cut the cheese slices into 3X4-inch rectangles.
3. Spread approximately 1 tablespoon chilled liver sausage mixture evenly on the cheese.

4. Roll the cheese and filling, then skewer with a cellophane-tipped toothpick.
5. Refrigerate until serving time.

SPECIAL HINTS
For variety, dip the ends of each roll in mayonnaise and then in a combination of finely chopped walnuts and sweet basil.

Pickled Tongue Roll-em-ups

Yields 30 roll-em-ups.

The rippling edges of escarole peek brightly out of this substantial meat roll. The piquant mustard and crisp pickle are excellent complements to the savory tongue.

INGREDIENTS
¼ cup garlic-flavored bread crumbs
¼ cup prepared mustard
1 head escarole (see Special Hints)
30 slices pickled tongue
30 miniature sweet gherkin pickles

SPECIAL EQUIPMENT
Cellophane-tipped toothpicks

INSTRUCTIONS
1. Combine the bread crumbs with the mustard.
2. Tear the escarole into bite-sized pieces.
3. Spread the mustard mixture evenly on all the tongue slices. Top with the escarole and a pickle.
4. Make a tight, firm roll and secure it through the center with a cellophane-tipped toothpick.
5. Refrigerate until serving time.

SPECIAL HINTS
Escarole is suggested here for its decorative ripply effect. Feel free, however, to use any variety of lettuce.

Prosciutto-Cantaloupe Sticks

Yields 30 sticks.

That elegant combination of prosciutto and melon makes a refreshing new impact with the addition of almonds and cream cheese. These crunchy roll-em-ups disappear fast, so make plenty.

INGREDIENTS

1 large cantaloupe
½ cup slivered almonds
1 teaspoon ground nutmeg
8 ounces cream cheese, softened
15 slices prosciutto ham

SPECIAL EQUIPMENT

Cellophane-tipped toothpicks.

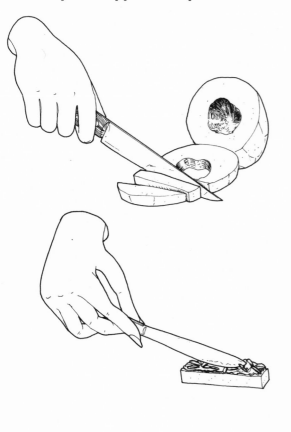

INSTRUCTIONS

1. Cut cantaloupe in half, discard the seeds and remove the rind.
2. To fashion cantaloupe sticks, cut crosswise slices approximately 1 inch wide. Lay each slice flat and cut into long slices about 1 inch wide. Trim off the curved ends, and you have cantaloupe sticks.
3. These sticks can be cut to any desired length, but I suggest 3-inch pieces for convenient handling.
4. Mix the almonds and nutmeg into the cream cheese.
5. Spread approximately 1 teaspoon of the cream cheese mixture on one side of each cantaloupe stick.
6. Cut each prosciutto slice in half. Wrap a prosciutto slice around each melon stick and fasten with a cellophane-tipped toothpick.
7. Refrigerate until serving time.

SPECIAL HINTS

Cut any leftover cantaloupe sticks into cubes and skewer them with a cellophane-tipped toothpick for a refreshing snack, or toss them into a fruit salad.

Ham and Cheese Bugles

Strike a happy high note at any party with ham and cheese "bugles." Rest assured the only sound you'll hear from guests is "more." These tasty hors d'oeuvres can also double for child-sized luncheon fare, where food must be fun to eat as well as nutritious.

INGREDIENTS

8 4X4 sandwich slices white bread
1 cup minced onion
1 cup spreadable sharp Cheddar
  cheese
½ teaspoon celery seed
Freshly ground pepper to taste
30 thin slices ham

SPECIAL EQUIPMENT
Cellophane-tipped toothpicks

INSTRUCTIONS

1. Toast the white bread. Trim off the crusts.
2. Combine the minced onion with the Cheddar cheese. Add the celery seed and pepper and mix well.
3. Spread the mixture generously on the toasted bread slices.
4. Slice the bread into 1-inch-wide strips. Trim the ham slices to fit the length of the bread strips.
5. Roll a thin ham slice around each bread strip and fasten with a cellophane-tipped toothpick.
6. Refrigerate until serving time.

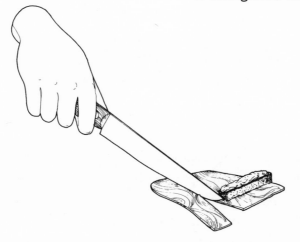

Six

❧ Toothpick Tidbits

❧ For those who love to entertain but have limited time, these hasty tasties come together quickly yet elegantly. Here's a chapter full of easy recipes that add an exciting new dimension to cold cuts and cheeses. Ordinary foods and leftovers are transformed into elegant envelopes, colorful cubes, classic kabobs. There's even a flavorful bacon flowerpot. Toothpick tidbits are easy on the budget, too.

Clever hors d'oeuvre chefs can plan ahead for special occasions by freezing leftover roast beef, ham or turkey after family feasts. Then when it's party time, thaw meat completely and proceed with the recipe. Packaged cold cuts make delicious hors d'oeuvres, and their uniform size and shape allow for convenient cutting and professional-looking results.

All of these tasty tidbits are skewered with cellophane-tipped toothpicks, the magic touch that adds festivity to familiar favorites. Hors d'oeuvre trays ablaze with feathery colors belie the quick and inexpensive preparation.

ARTIST'S NOTE

To assemble an eye-pleasing platter of cold cuts begin by placing a layer of lettuce or other fresh greenery on a platter. Arrange a layer of overlapping cold cuts in a circle on top of lettuce. Fold salami slices in half to comprise the second layer and angle cheese slices on top of the salami for the third layer. Repeat the sequence one or two times if you desire staggered layers. Top with carrot and cold cut curls skewered with toothpicks into lettuce. Serve chilled with bread and condiments.

Tuna Envelopes

Yields 30 envelopes.

Tuna salad is sandwiched in toasted bread and topped with a tangy pineapple cube to make an easy pick-up. Quick and clever, tuna never had it so good!

INGREDIENTS

1 recipe Tuna Salad, page 162
½ cup butter, softened
½ teaspoon dried dill
30 slices white bread
30 cubes pineapple, well drained

SPECIAL EQUIPMENT

Cellophane-tipped toothpicks

INSTRUCTIONS

1. Prepare 2 cups of tuna salad.
2. Blend the butter and dill.
3. Trim crusts from bread. Lightly toast the bread slices. Flatten each slightly with a rolling pin and cut into 3X3-inch squares.
4. Spread each square with dill butter. Next spread 1 to 1½ tablespoons of tuna salad evenly to all corners of the bread.
5. Fold the bread into a triangle by bringing the diagonal corners together. Insert a cellophane-tipped toothpick through a pineapple cube and skewer through the center of the triangle.

SPECIAL HINTS

Be sure to drain the pineapple well to avoid soggy sandwiches.

ARTIST'S NOTE

For variety, fold the envelopes into rectangles by folding edges together rather than diagonal corners.

DO-AHEAD NOTE

Prepare the tuna envelopes, including the garnish, several hours before serving. Refrigerate in a single layer and serve chilled.

B-L-T Tidbits

B-L-T tidbits are miniature versions of the famed bacon, lettuce and tomato sandwich. Skewer, slice and serve!

INGREDIENTS

½ cup mayonnaise

¼ cup sweet pickle relish, well-drained

8 slices white bread

16 strips of bacon

4 lettuce leaves

4 slices cheese—Swiss, Cheddar or
  Monterey Jack

12 thin slices of tomato

30 cocktail onions

SPECIAL EQUIPMENT

Cellophane-tipped toothpicks

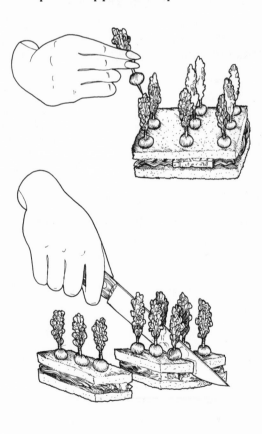

INSTRUCTIONS

1. Combine the mayonnaise and relish.
2. Toast the white bread and spread slices generously with the mayonnaise-relish mixture.
3. Fry the bacon until crisp. Drain well on paper towels.
4. Place the bacon slices side by side on 4 pieces of toasted bread, covering the entire surface.
5. Top the layer of bacon with a lettuce leaf and slice of cheese. Cover with a layer of tomatoes. (Don't worry about overlap, as it will be trimmed off.) Top with another toast slice.
6. Trim the crusts off the sandwich and mentally divide it into 9 1-inch squares. Skewer a cocktail onion on a cellophane-tipped toothpick and insert through each imaginary square.
7. Make 3 equidistant vertical slices, keeping the sandwich together. Make 3 equidistant horizontal slices to form 9 cubes, and serve.

SPECIAL HINTS

To prevent the tidbits from becoming soggy, purchase firm tomatoes, and drain the pickle relish well.

DO-AHEAD NOTE

Prepare the sandwich several hours ahead of time but do not cut or garnish. Store, wrapped in foil, in the refrigerator. Just before serving, heat the foil-wrapped sandwiches until warm, then garnish and cut into cubes.

Mandarin Ham Kabobs

There's a subtle hint of the Orient in these simple mandarin orange and sweet-and-sour ham kabobs. Your guests will never dream the whole preparation took just a few minutes.

INGREDIENTS

1 cup butter
4 slices white bread, ½ inch thick
3 tablespoons vinegar
½ teaspoon dry mustard
¼ teaspoon powdered ginger
½ teaspoon ground cloves
3½ tablespoons orange marmalade
36 cubes cooked ham, 1X1X½ inch
2 small cans mandarin orange sections,
   well drained

SPECIAL EQUIPMENT

Cellophane-tipped toothpicks

INSTRUCTIONS

1. Melt ½ cup of the butter in a skillet. Trim the crusts off the bread and fry the slices in the melted butter until they are light brown on both sides.
2. Drain them well on absorbent paper towels.
3. Cut fried bread into 1-inch squares. Each 4X4-inch bread slice yields 9 squares.
3. To make the sauce, melt the remaining ¼ cup butter in the same skillet. While the butter is melting, in a small mixing bowl, combine vinegar, mustard, ginger, cloves and orange marmalade. Mix well and blend this mixture into the melted butter, stirring thoroughly.
4. Add the ham cubes to the sauce and simmer gently for approximately 5 minutes.
5. On a cellophane-tipped toothpick, skewer a mandarin orange section, a ham cube, another mandarin orange section and finally a fried bread cube.
6. Serve while the meat is hot, or refrigerate the kabobs until party time and serve cold.

DO-AHEAD NOTE

Assemble the kabobs complete with the mandarin orange garnish several hours before serving time and refrigerate.

SERVING SUGGESTIONS

Reserve any remaining sauce to be used as a dip with the kabobs. This sauce is popular and goes quickly, so you may want to make extra.

Roast Beef Spirals

Yields 36 spirals.

Spirals of roast beef and cream cheese have a delicious effect on your guests. Best of all, they're easy as can be.

INGREDIENTS

16 ounces cream cheese, softened
2 garlic cloves, minced
1 teaspoon ground ginger
6 slices roast beef, cut ¼ inch thick
9 canned spiced crab apples, well
    drained and quartered

SPECIAL EQUIPMENT

Blender (optional)
Cellophane-tipped toothpicks

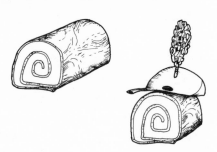

INSTRUCTIONS

1. Prepare the filling by combining the cream cheese, garlic and ginger. Whip in a blender.
2. Spread the filling generously and evenly on the roast beef slices and roll them up lengthwise. Wrap the rolls in foil and freeze them for half an hour.
3. Remove rolls from the freezer and cut into 1-inch-wide slices, which will have a lovely spiral design.
4. Garnish each slice with a quartered crab apple attached with a cellophane-tipped toothpick and serve.

DO-AHEAD NOTE

Prepare the rolls the day before and freeze. Two hours before serving, remove from the freezer. Cut, garnish and allow to stand at room temperature until serving time.

Cheese-Bacon Flowerpots

Yields 30 flowerpots.

What has green leaves, a golden brown blossom, comes in a flowerpot and tastes delicious? Your soon-to-be favorite hors d'oeuvre. These delightful tidbits flower with the flavors of bacon and cheese.

INGREDIENTS

15 strips of bacon
16 ounces hard, sharp cheese, such as
    Cheddar or Swiss
30 large pitted green olives

INSTRUCTIONS

1. Fry the bacon until it is brown but not crisp. With two forks roll each strip tightly. Continue frying the bacon rolls until they are crisp. Drain rolls thoroughly on paper towels. Then cut each bacon

SPECIAL EQUIPMENT
Plain rounded toothpicks

roll in half to create 2 smaller rolls.

2. Cut the cheese into 1-inch cubes.

3. Slice each green olive in half lengthwise for the leaves.

4. To assemble the flowerpot, insert a toothpick halfway into the cheese. Skewer the two olive halves onto the toothpick, pointing each half in opposite directions to simulate leaves.

5. Top with the bacon-roll flower and serve.

DO-AHEAD NOTE
Cube the cheese and fry the bacon into flowers the day before. Refrigerate the bacon separately in foil for convenient party-time reheating.

Cold-Cut Ribbons

Yields approximately 30 ribbons.

Layers of ordinary cold cuts and American cheese suddenly become an elegant and tempting hors d'oeuvre when spiced with a tangy cream cheese spread. These colorful rectangles make geometry delicious.

INGREDIENTS
16 ounces cream cheese, softened
¾ cup minced onion
1 tablespoon mustard
5 packages (4 ounces each) any square
   cold cut or luncheon meat
4 packages (6 ounces each) American
   cheese slices
15 miniature sweet gherkin pickles,
   sliced in half lengthwise

SPECIAL EQUIPMENT
Cellophane-tipped toothpicks

INSTRUCTIONS
1. Prepare the spread by combining the cream cheese, onion and mustard.

2. Lightly spread the cream cheese mixture on one slice of meat, top with a slice of American cheese, then more cream cheese and another slice of meat. Repeat the process until the stacks includes 3 layers of meat and 2 layers of American cheese with cream cheese in between.

3. Freeze the cold-cut stacks uncut for approximately 1 hour. When the stacks are firm, cut them into 1X2-inch ribbon strips.

4. Center a pickle slice on each cold-cut ribbon. Skewer through the center with a cellophane-tipped toothpick and serve.

For variety, combine several kinds of meats and sliced cheeses in one 4X4-inch stack.
Cut the stacks into different shapes, such as triangles and rounds.

DO-AHEAD NOTE

Prepare the cold-cut stacks a day in advance. Freeze them ungarnished in foil. Remove the stacks from the freezer and thaw at room temperature. Cut into ribbons, add the garnish and refrigerate or serve.

Salami Wedges

Yields 32 wedges.

These spicy wedges have a surprising crunch that stimulates your guests' curiosity and inspires frequent returns to the hors d'oeuvre table.

INGREDIENTS

16 ounces spreadable Cheddar cheese
½ cup chopped walnuts
24 slices of hard salami, 3 inches in diameter
32 cocktail onions

SPECIAL EQUIPMENT

Cellophane-tipped toothpicks

INSTRUCTIONS

1. Combine spreadable Cheddar cheese with chopped walnuts.
2. Spread the cheese mixture on a slice of salami. Top with another salami slice. Spread the mixture on that slice and top with a third slice of salami. Repeat, building stacks with the remaining cheese mixture and salami.
3. Wrap the layered meat stacks in foil and freeze for approximately 1 hour.
4. Remove the stacks from the freezer and cut each stack into 4 equal wedges. Attach a cocktail onion to each salami wedge with a cellophane-tipped toothpick.

DO-AHEAD NOTE

Wrap the uncut salami stacks securely in foil, then freeze. Thaw at room temperature. Cut into wedges and refrigerate or serve.

Seven

🌿 Eggs Wonderful Eggs

🌿 Could Mother Nature have known what a gourmet blessing she gave us in the hen? Eggs really are wonderful. What other food is so nutritious yet versatile? There is magic hidden within their fragile shells. You'll be amazed as numerous varieties of hors d'oeuvres hatch from eggs as you pickle, batik and stuff them. What hen would believe her eggs could produce edible swans? With some ingenuity and shrimp, you can make it happen. Some eggs will even resemble floral cameos, complete with edible frames. The egg hors d'oeuvres are beautiful, but best of all, they're easy to prepare, and they taste delicious.

To ensure perfect eggs, keep in mind some simple suggestions. First, none but the freshest eggs will do. To be sure, purchase those with rough shells (those with smooth shells tend to be older). Buy only eggs that have been refrigerated. These recipes are geared to medium-size eggs. At home, store them in their own carton to protect them from absorbing odors right through their shells. The color of the shell, incidentally, is determined by the breed of the hen and does not affect the nutritional value, taste or artistry of our egg hors d'oeuvres.

Many people overlook the most important part of fashioning beautiful, tasty egg dishes—the cooking. A hard-cooked egg that has been properly prepared has a bright yellow yolk and a tender white. Since eye appeal and good taste are the major goals of hors d'oeuvre making, do pay special attention to my instructions on how to hard-cook an egg. You'll notice that I say *hard-cook* rather than *hard-boil*. That's because there is actually little boiling time involved. The water should be boiling slowly when the eggs, at room temperature, are added. Gently submerge the eggs in the boiling water using a spoon or an egg basket. Immediately reduce the heat to a simmer and cook the eggs for 15 to 20 minutes. Peel immediately to prevent discoloration and cover with water to store.

To prevent prepared egg hors d'oeuvres from sliding around on your serving tray, shave a thin slice of the egg white off the bottom to give the egg a flat, stable resting surface.

Since the egg white is such a versatile container, just about any filling can be delightful. You'll want to experiment with ingredients to find your favorite combinations. The recipes in this section list the basic ingredients, but allow for your personal taste when it comes to proportions. Blend and taste, you can't go wrong!

DO-AHEAD NOTE

For convenience, eggs may be hard-cooked several days in advance, the filling prepared the day before use and the garnishes artfully applied just prior to serving.

Shrimp Butterfly Eggs
Yields 30 butterflies.

A tray of colorful shrimp butterflies will lift the spirits and appetites of your guests, for these butterflies actually have wings.

INGREDIENTS

15 hard-cooked eggs
½ teaspoon dill
Garlic salt to taste
4 to 5 tablespoons mayonnaise
30 small to medium cooked shrimp, shelled and deveined
4-ounce can pimiento strips

INSTRUCTIONS

1. Slice the hard-cooked eggs in half lengthwise and remove the yolks.
2. In a small bowl, mix the yolks with the dill, garlic salt and just enough mayonnaise to create a thick paste.
3. With a spreader, fill each egg white, leaving a smooth surface.
4. Slice the shrimp on the inside of the curve, being careful not to cut completely through. Flatten the opened side of the shrimp with the flat side of a knife. This spreads the "wings" of the shrimp butterfly.
5. Place a shrimp butterfly in the middle of each stuffed egg.
6. Place a tiny strip of pimiento on the center seam between the butterfly wings, and the butterfly seems to take flight. Refrigerate until serving time.

ARTIST'S NOTE

For an especially artful effect, place the shrimp on the egg at a slight angle.

Pickled Pink Eggs

You needn't wait for Easter to have colored eggs, and these beautiful pink ones, delectably pickled in your own homemade brine, don't take hours to make. They're so easy, and you can store them in the refrigerator, ready to delight surprised guests or to brighten up an impromptu picnic.

INGREDIENTS

2 cups water
1 ½ cups distilled vinegar
1 clove fresh garlic, crushed
2 ½ tablespoons sugar
¼ teaspoon ground ginger
½ teaspoon celery seed
1 bay leaf
½ teaspoon dried tarragon
3 or 4 slices raw fresh beet
12 hard-cooked eggs in their shells

SPECIAL EQUIPMENT

Glass or ceramic jar with a tight-fitting lid. An airtight container especially designed for pickling works best, but is not essential.

INSTRUCTIONS

1. To make the brine, combine all the ingredients except the eggs in the container in which the eggs will be stored.
2. For an unusual design, partially crack the shells of 6 of the eggs and submerge them, in their shells, in the pickling liquid. When the eggs are later peeled, the effect is striking, closely resembling a batik design. Peel the remaining eggs and place them in the solution, too.
3. Pickle eggs in the refrigerator for at least 2 days.
4. Present the eggs on a large platter surrounded by fresh greenery.

SPECIAL HINTS

Pickled eggs can be kept refrigerated for several weeks in the pickling brine. The vinegar preserves the eggs and keeps them tasty.

The sliced beet provides wonderful color and can be eaten along with the eggs or used as a decorative garnish.

Crisscross Eggs

Yields 30 to 36 egg halves.

Crisscross eggs are particularly colorful as well as taste pleasing. The buttery-smooth filling is rich and appetizing.

INGREDIENTS
18 hard-cooked eggs
Onion salt to taste
4 to 5 tablespoons butter, softened
½ cup tomato paste
Few drops of Tabasco sauce

SPECIAL EQUIPMENT
Pastry bag with writing tip

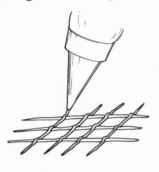

INSTRUCTIONS
1. Cut the eggs lengthwise. Remove the yolks and reserving 3, place them in a mixing bowl.
2. Add onion salt and just enough softened butter to make a thick paste. Mix until smooth.
3. Spread the yolk filling on the egg whites, leaving a smooth, flat surface.
4. Mix the reserved yolks with the tomato paste and Tabasco.
5. Fill a writing-tipped pastry bag with the tomato-egg paste and decorate the top of the egg in a crisscross pattern.
6. Refrigerate until serving time.

Caviar Grape Eggs

Yields 30 egg halves.

This egg design whimsically features caviar beautifully clustered like grapes as a garnish for deviled eggs.

INGREDIENTS
15 hard-cooked eggs
4 to 5 tablespoons sour cream
Garlic salt to taste
2 ounces red or black caviar
Parsley

SPECIAL EQUIPMENT
Pastry bag with star tip

INSTRUCTIONS
1. Cut the eggs in half lengthwise and remove the yolks.
2. In a small bowl, mash the egg yolks with a fork. Add just enough sour cream to the yolks to make a thick paste. Season with garlic salt.
3. Place the egg yolk mixture in a star-tipped pastry bag and pipe the mixture generously into the egg halves.

4. To garnish, gently spoon black or red caviar onto the center of each egg, shaping it into a cluster resembling a bunch of grapes. The tiny bunch should taper to a point.

5. Place a small sprig of parsley at the widest end of the caviar cluster to simulate leaves.

6. Refrigerate until serving time.

SPECIAL HINTS

For best results, garnish these eggs close to serving time.

Egg Swans

Yields 30 swans.

Your guests will think you spent hours making these beautiful little swans, when actually they're easy, fast and always spectacular. No one will know but you and I!

INGREDIENTS

1 cup finely chopped cooked shrimp, shelled and deveined

½ teaspoon dill

Garlic powder to taste

2 to 3 tablespoons mayonnaise-style salad dressing

15 hard-cooked eggs

30 small to medium cooked shrimp, shelled and deveined

Fresh parsley

SPECIAL EQUIPMENT

Cellophane-tipped toothpicks

INSTRUCTIONS

1. For the filling, combine the chopped shrimp, dill and garlic powder to taste with enough salad dressing to moisten the mixture.

2. Slice hard-cooked eggs in half lengthwise. Remove the yolks and store for another use.

3. Generously mound the shrimp mixture into the egg white.

4. To make the swan's neck, hold the whole shrimp at the curved tip. Run a toothpick down through it to straighten. Attach it to the egg by skewering it into the wide end of the egg.

5. Make tail feathers with a sprig of parsley.

6. Refrigerate until serving time.

DO-AHEAD NOTE

Fashion the shrimp that form the swan necks ahead of time for fast assembly.

Pink Ladies

These Pink Ladies won't pack the inebriating punch of the alcoholic kind, but they will dazzle your guests and keep them coming back for more. These charming and colorful egg cups are equally at home at a luncheon or a grand buffet.

INGREDIENTS

12 to 15 Pickled Pink Eggs, page 71
½ recipe (1 cup) Potato Salad, page 162
1 small jar sliced pickled beets

SPECIAL EQUIPMENT

Pastry bag with star tip
Aspic cutters

INSTRUCTIONS

1. Cut pickled eggs in half crosswise.
2. Remove yolks and add 3 or 4 to the potato salad. Reserve the rest for use in other recipes.
3. With tiny aspic cutters, cut decorative shapes out of the pickled beets.
4. Whip potato salad in a blender or food processor until thick and smooth.
5. Fill a star-tipped pastry bag with the whipped potato mixture and generously fill the center of the egg halves.
6. Encircle the potato salad with the tiny pickled beet cutouts.
7. Refrigerate until serving time.

SPECIAL HINTS

You might want to use your own favorite potato salad for this design, or the store-bought variety works beautifully, too.

CAMEO EGGS

These flowery egg designs look like miniature cameos of flowers, complete with the traditional oval frame. Actually, they're egg halves filled with a variety of piquant egg yolk combinations, artfully garnished and served in their own edible frames.

Carrot Flower Cameos

Yields 30 cameos.

INGREDIENTS

15 hard-cooked eggs

3 to 4 tablespoons mayonnaise

1 to 2 tablespoons chopped anchovies or anchovy paste

2 small carrots, peeled and parboiled until just tender

8 to 10 pitted black olives, slivered

INSTRUCTIONS

1. Cut the hard-cooked eggs in half lengthwise and remove yolks.

2. To make filling, mix yolks and enough mayonnaise to form a thick paste. Add anchovies and mix well.

3. Fill the egg whites with the yolk mixture, leaving a smooth surface. Spread a thin coating of mayonnaise over the egg filling.

4. Slice carrots very thin. To make the flower, overlap carrot slices in a circle on the wide portion of the egg halves. Arrange olive slivers below the flower to form stem and leaves. The slices of vegetable will adhere to the mayonnaise coating.

5. Refrigerate until serving time.

Salmon Bud Cameos

Yields 30 cameos.

INGREDIENTS

15 hard-cooked eggs

1 teaspoon dill

4 to 5 tablespoons cream cheese

Mayonnaise

2 to 3 thin slices smoked salmon

1 scallion

INSTRUCTIONS

1. Cut hard-cooked eggs lengthwise and remove yolks.

2. In a mixing bowl combine yolks with dill and add enough cream cheese to form a smooth paste.

3. Fill the egg whites with the yolk mixture, leaving a smooth surface. Spread a thin coat of mayonnaise on the filling.

4. To fashion the salmon rosebuds, cut salmon slices ½ inch wide and 1 inch long. Roll up tightly. Cluster 2 or 3 buds in the center of the egg to form a bouquet. Press buds firmly into egg filling.

5. Fashion delicate leaves from the green of the scallion and arrange them around the rosebuds.

6. Refrigerate until serving time.

SPECIAL HINTS
The more tightly you roll the salmon, the smaller
and more delicate the buds will be.

DO-AHEAD NOTE
Fashion the salmon rosebuds and leaves ahead of
time for speedy assembly.

Flowering Ham Cameos

Yields 30 cameos.

INGREDIENTS
15 hard-cooked eggs
1 tablespoon chopped fresh chives
4 to 5 tablespoons mayonnaise
3 thin slices ham
30 pitted green olives

INSTRUCTIONS
1. Cut eggs in half lengthwise and remove yolks.
2. Prepare the filling by mixing egg yolks with
chives and enough mayonnaise to create a thick,
smooth paste.
3. Fill the egg whites with the yolk mixture and
smooth with a spreader. Then add a thin coating of
mayonnaise.
4. Cut each ham slice into 5 strips ½ inch wide and
2 inches long. Fashion flowers by rolling ham strips
tightly (see Garnishes, page 166). To fashion olive
flowerpot, see Garnishes, page 166.
5. Place a ham rose at the top of the wide end of
each egg half. Place the olive stem and flowerpot
under the flower.
6. Refrigerate until serving time.

DO AHEAD NOTE
Fashion the ham rose, flowerpot and leaves ahead
of time for speedy assembly.

Tomato Rosette Cameos

Yields 30 cameos.

INGREDIENTS

15 hard-cooked eggs
4 to 5 tablespoons mayonnaise
30 small cherry tomatoes
1 small green pepper
3¾-ounce can skinless and boneless
    sardines, drained and mashed

SPECIAL EQUIPMENT
Leaf-shaped aspic cutter

INSTRUCTIONS

1. Cut eggs in half lengthwise and remove yolks.
2. To prepare the filling, mash the egg yolks and mix with enough mayonnaise to moisten. Add mashed sardines to taste and mix thoroughly.
3. Fill the egg whites with this mixture, leaving a smooth surface. Spread with a thin coating of mayonnaise.
4. Fashion tomato rosettes from cherry tomatoes and leaves from green pepper (see Garnishes, pages 165 and 166, respectively).
5. Place a tomato rosette in the center of each filled egg half.
6. Arrange green pepper leaves around rosette.
7. Refrigerate until serving time.

DO-AHEAD NOTE

Fashion the tomato rosettes in advance, for speedy assembly.

Cheese Daisy Cameos

Yields 30 cameos.

INGREDIENTS

15 hard-cooked eggs
4 to 5 tablespoons mayonnaise
2 tablespoons minced onion
3 to 4 thin slices Cheddar cheese
30 capers
Fresh chives or scallion

SPECIAL EQUIPMENT
Leaf-shaped aspic cutter

INSTRUCTIONS

1. Cut eggs in half lengthwise and remove yolks.
2. In a small bowl, mash the egg yolks with a fork. Add enough mayonnaise to moisten and mix until smooth. Blend in the minced onion.
3. Fill the egg whites with the yolk mixture. Level to form a smooth surface. Spread a thin coating of mayonnaise over the filling.
4. Form the daisy petals by cutting the cheese with a leaf-shaped aspic cutter.

5. Fashion the cheese petals in the shape of a daisy at the wide portion of the egg. Dot the center with a caper.

6. Cut the chives or green part of the scallion to desired stem length and position them down the center of the egg.

7. Refrigerate until serving time.

DO-AHEAD NOTE

Fashion the cheese petals ahead of time.

STUFFED EGG CUPS

Your guests will be delighted if these cups runneth over—the more filling, the better. These variations on the celebrated stuffed egg feature enticing hot or cold fillings that need little more than a hint of garnish to look and taste sensational.

Egg cups are cut crosswise to take advantage of the deepest hollow in the egg, but there are many cutting variations that will change the cup's appearance completely and add variety to your hors d'oeuvre tray.

CARVING VARIATIONS

Zigzag: With a narrow-blade paring knife, make an angled incision about halfway into the egg. Pull the knife out and make another incision, forming a *V*. Proceed to make adjoining *V*'s around the circumference of the egg, making sure the points meet. When you have cut all the way around, the two halves should separate, each with a zig-

zag. (*Hint:* To zigzag easily, place the peeled egg in an egg cup for stability while cutting.)

Fluted: To flute the tops of the egg halves, use a ripple-edged knife. Make one clean cut through the egg, crosswise or lengthwise. Whichever way you cut the top of the egg halves, do remember to shave a small slice from the bottom, so the egg will not slide and will stand upright on the serving tray.

Salmon Egg Cups

Yields 30 egg cups.

The contrast of sweet and salty gives this egg dish its unique flavor. I have found this to be one of the favorite egg cups, so have plenty on hand.

INGREDIENTS

15 hard-cooked eggs
7¾-ounce can salmon, flaked
4 ounces cream cheese, softened
2 tablespoons finely chopped walnuts
1 tablespoon honey
Garlic powder to taste
Fresh parsley

SPECIAL EQUIPMENT

Ripple-edged knife
Pastry bag with star tip (optional)

INSTRUCTIONS

1. Slice egg lengthwise with a ripple-edged knife. Remove yolks and save for another recipe.
2. In a mixing bowl, combine salmon with cream cheese. Add finely chopped walnuts, honey and a dash of garlic powder to taste. Mix well.
3. Spoon or pipe the mixture into the egg whites.
4. Garnish with a tiny sprig of parsley for color.
5. Refrigerate until serving time.

Shrimp Cup

Yields 30 egg cups.

INGREDIENTS

15 hard-cooked eggs
2 tablespoons butter
1 cup chopped cooked shrimp
1 garlic clove, crushed
Fresh lemon juice to taste
¼ teaspoon sweet basil
Tabasco sauce
¼ teaspoon grated lemon peel
1 tablespoon sauterne (optional)

SPECIAL EQUIPMENT

Ripple-edged knife

INSTRUCTIONS

1. Prepare the hard-cooked eggs by cutting them in half lengthwise with a ripple-edged knife. Remove the yolks and store for other uses.
2. Melt butter in a skillet. Add shrimp, garlic, a touch of lemon juice, sweet basil, Tabasco and grated lemon peel.
3. Cook gently for about 2 minutes to blend flavors.
4. Add sauterne just before turning off the heat.
5. When the mixture is hot (and you're tempted to nibble from the pan), spoon it generously into the egg cups.
6. Serve hot or keep on a warming tray.

Chicken Liver Egg Cups

Yields 30 cups.

INGREDIENTS

15 hard-cooked eggs
3 tablespoons olive oil
2 tablespoons finely chopped shallots
1 cup (about ½ pound) fresh chicken
  livers, finely chopped
½ teaspoon sweet basil
2 tablespoons sauterne
2 tablespoons crushed onion-flavored
  croutons

INSTRUCTIONS

1. Prepare the eggs by cutting crosswise in a zigzag design. Reserve the yolks for other uses.
2. Sauté the shallots in the olive oil until transparent.
3. Add the chicken livers, basil and sauterne to the pan and cook until livers are firm but still slightly pink inside.
4. Just before removing the mixture from the pan, add the crushed onion croutons. Stir several times.
5. Spoon the mixture into the egg cups. Serve hot.

Bacon and Egg Cups

Yields 30 egg cups.

INGREDIENTS

15 hard-cooked eggs
½ cup crumbled cooked bacon
¾ cup pimiento-flavored cream
  cheese, softened
Garlic powder to taste

SPECIAL EQUIPMENT
Ripple-edged knife

INSTRUCTIONS

1. Cut the eggs crosswise with a ripple-edged knife. Remove egg yolks and reserve for use in another recipe.
2. Mix the bacon with the cream cheese. Add a touch of garlic powder to taste.
3. Fill the egg whites with heaping spoonfuls of the mixture.
4. Refrigerate until serving time.

Eight

❧ From the Sea

❧ Marine delights such as shrimp, crab, oysters and lobster are stuffed with a creamy filling, nestled in a miniature tart shell, rolled in bread, even tucked into tiny scallop sand dollars. Sometimes they are baked, other times they are fried. Elegant wrappings, sumptuous sauces, mild cheeses and interesting spices are called into play to highlight the enchanting flavors of nature's own precious treats.

When you start out with such succulent raw materials, it is hard not to succeed. There is something for everyone in this chapter; so experiment with the recipes and have fun! If you are a seafood lover like me, you just can't seem to get enough of the ocean's bountiful offerings. Once you have sampled a few of these recipes, you may be inspired to combine ideas from several of the dishes and invent your own unique and delectable seafood specialties!

DO-AHEAD NOTE

These hors d'oeuvres may be prepared—even fried or baked—ahead of time and then frozen in a single layer. Reheat them in the oven just before serving.

Hot Crab Tartlets

Yields 30 tartlets.

An extraordinary offering, combining the best of land and sea! Bread tart shells are stuffed with crab meat, cream cheese and onions, then baked and sprinkled with bits of pimiento.

INGREDIENTS

30 Bread Tartlet Shells, page 104
1 cup chopped crabmeat
4 ounces cream cheese, softened
3 tablespoons minced onion
Tabasco sauce to taste
½ teaspoon garlic powder
3 tablespoons minced pimiento

INSTRUCTIONS

1. Combine the crabmeat and cream cheese in a mixing bowl.
2. Add the onion, Tabasco and garlic powder and mix until well blended.
3. Place 1 tablespoon of the filling in each tartlet.
4. Bake the crab tartlets for 10 minutes in a 350 degree oven.
5. Sprinkle with minced pimiento and serve hot.

Cheese-Oyster Tarts

Yields 30 tarts.

Succulent smoked oysters are mixed with garlic bread crumbs and Swiss cheese, then nestled atop bread tartlets and gently baked to yield a wonderful taste combination.

INGREDIENTS

1 cup smoked oysters,chopped
½ cup garlic-flavored bread crumbs
1/3 cup shredded Swiss cheese
30 Bread Tartlet Shells, page 104

INSTRUCTIONS

1. Combine oysters, bread crumbs and cheese.
2. Place a teaspoonful of the mixture in each tartlet.
3. Bake at 350 degrees approximately 10 minutes, until the cheese melts. Serve hot.

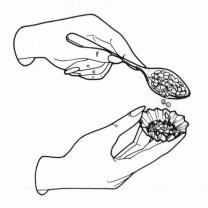

Fried Clam Rolls

Yields 32 rolls.

Lovers of clams will appreciate this anything-but-routine version. Clams are mixed with dill, Tabasco and butter, then rolled in white bread and deep-fried to a golden brown.

INGREDIENTS

½ cup butter, softened
1 beaten egg
1 teaspoon dill
½ teaspoon garlic powder
1¼ cups minced cooked clams
6 drops Tabasco sauce
1 teaspoon lemon juice
16 slices of white bread
Oil for deep frying

INSTRUCTIONS

1. In a mixing bowl combine butter, egg, dill, garlic powder, clams, Tabasco and lemon juice. Mix thoroughly.
2. Trim the crusts from the bread. Using a rolling pin flatten the slices until they are thin.
3. Place approximately 1 tablespoon of the clam mixture on each bread slice, spreading it from end to end. Then roll tightly.
4. Heat the oil to 360 degrees, or until a drop of egg bubbles to the top. Deep-fry the rolls until they are golden brown.
5. Drain on paper towels and cut each roll in half. Serve hot.

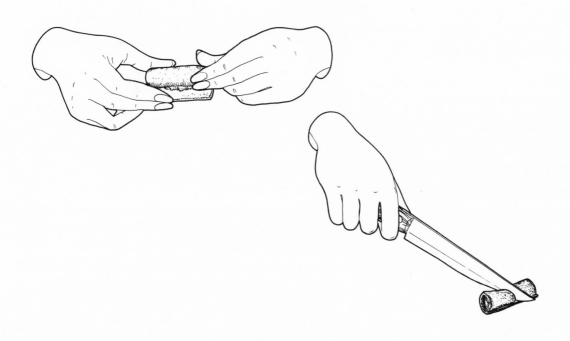

Escargot Tartlets

Though hardly from the sea, the snail, with its hard outer shell, seems closely linked with the seafood kingdom. Its delicate flavor combines with sautéed mushrooms, chives and fresh garlic to form a rich, elegant filling for bread tarts.

INGREDIENTS

½ cup butter
4 cloves garlic, minced
¾ cup finely chopped snail meat
½ cup finely chopped mushrooms
1 tablespoon chopped chives
30 Bread Tartlet Shells, page 104

INSTRUCTIONS

1. Melt butter in a small skillet. Add the garlic, snail meat, mushrooms and chives and sauté over medium heat for 5 minutes.
2. Place bread tart shells on an ungreased baking sheet. Spoon snail filling mixture into each bread tart shell.
3. Bake in a 350-degree oven for 10 minutes. Serve the escargot tartlets while hot and juicy.

Fried Shrimp Squares

Freshly grated ginger adds zest to this tempting combination of chopped fresh shrimp and egg on toast. Deep fried upside-down to a golden brown, these squares are irresistible.

INGREDIENTS

8 slices firm white bread, toasted
1½ cups chopped raw shrimp, shelled
  and deveined
1 teaspoon freshly grated ginger root
2 beaten eggs
½ teaspoon sugar
½ teaspoon salt
Dash of pepper
1 tablespoon plus 1 teaspoon
  cornstarch
Oil for deep frying

INSTRUCTIONS

1. Remove the crusts from the bread and cut each slice into 4 squares.
2. In a mixing bowl, combine the shrimp, ginger root, eggs, sugar, salt, pepper and cornstarch.
3. Heat the oil to 360 degrees, or until a drop of egg bubbles to the top.
4. Generously spread the shrimp mixture on each bread square and fry, shrimp side down (the shrimp won't fall off), until golden on both sides.
5. Drain the shrimp squares on paper towels and serve hot.

DO-AHEAD NOTE

Prepare the shrimp squares according to the in-

structions. Allow to cool, then freeze in a single layer. At serving time, preheat the oven to 400 degrees and bake 10 minutes.

Seafood Crescents

Yields approximately 32 crescents.

These refrigerator roll turnovers, filled with a tasty blend of shrimp, anchovies, onions and Cheddar cheese, are sure to win applause from your guests.

INGREDIENTS

1 cup chopped cooked shrimp, shelled
  and deveined
½ cup spreadable Cheddar cheese
3 tablespoons chopped onion
2 tablespoons chopped anchovies
2 packages (8 ounces each)
  refrigerator crescent rolls

INSTRUCTIONS

1. In a mixing bowl, combine the shrimp, cheese, onion and anchovies. Mix until all ingredients are well blended.
2. Cut the crescent rolls where they are serrated, so that you have a triangle. Now cut each triangle in half again down the center.
3. Place a dab of the seafood mixture at the wide end of each refrigerator dough triangle. Roll toward the point. Pinch the ends together and curve them slightly to form a crescent.
4. Bake according to directions on the refrigerator roll package.

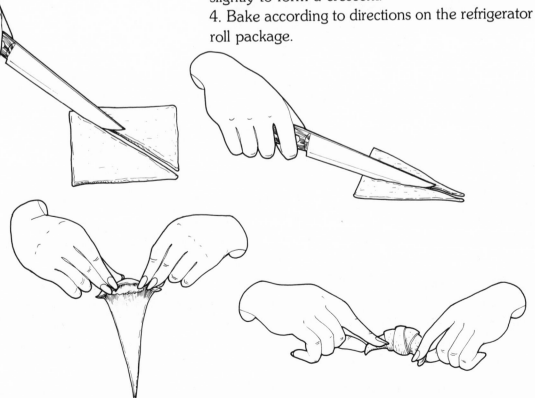

Salmon Won Ton Twists

Salmon, pineapple, cream cheese and spices create an imaginative filling for won ton skins. Deep fried and served hot, these twists are good to the very last bite!

INGREDIENTS

4 ounces cream cheese, softened
4-ounce can pink salmon, drained and
  flaked
1 teaspoon steak sauce
¼ teaspoon garlic powder
1 tablespoon chopped onion
¼ cup crushed pineapple, drained
2 tablespoons bread crumbs
12-ounce package won ton skins
Oil for deep frying

INSTRUCTIONS

1. Combine cream cheese, salmon, steak sauce, garlic powder, onion, pineapple and bread crumbs.
2. Place a won ton skin in front of you with one corner pointed toward you. Spoon 1 teaspoon of the salmon mixture onto the lower half of skin.
3. Roll the won ton skin away from you to form a cylinder. Seal the end with a small dab of water. Twist both ends to seal.
4. Heat oil to 360 degrees and deep-fry won tons approximately 1 minute, or until golden brown.
5. Drain on paper towels and serve hot.

Bacon-Wrapped Scallops

Your guests will call it rumaki from the sea, and they will come back for more when they taste the wonderful combination of scallops wrapped in bacon.

INGREDIENTS

1 cup lemon juice
½ teaspoon garlic powder
¼ cup butter
30 fresh scallops (cut in half if large)
15 strips of bacon
30 canned or fresh pineapple chunks

INSTRUCTIONS

1. Combine the lemon juice and garlic powder in a bowl. Marinate the scallops in this sauce for approximately ½ hour.
2. Melt butter in a frying pan. Pour scallops and lemon juice into the pan and simmer 10 minutes.
3. Remove scallops from liquid with a slotted

spoon and drain on paper towels.

4. Cut the bacon strips in half. Wrap a short strip of bacon around each scallop; then skewer through the center with a toothpick. Top it off with a pineapple chunk.

5. Broil the wrapped scallops, turning once, until the bacon is crisp. Serve hot with your favorite cocktail sauce.

Scallop Sand Dollars

Yields 30 dollars.

Reminiscent of sand dollars straight from the sea, these bread round look-alikes conceal a tasty filling of scallops and cheese, seasoned with dill and Worcestershire sauce.

INGREDIENTS

30 4X4 sandwich slices of white bread
2 cloves garlic, finely chopped
2 to 2½ tablespoons butter
½ teaspoon lemon juice
¼ teaspoon dill
1 cup chopped scallops
¼ teaspoon Worcestershire sauce
Salt and pepper to taste
½ cup freshly grated Parmesan cheese
Oil for deep frying

SPECIAL EQUIPMENT

2-inch round cookie cutter

INSTRUCTIONS

1. With the 2-inch round cookie cutter, cut 2 rounds from each bread slice.

2. Sauté the garlic in the butter for 1 minute. Add the lemon juice, dill, scallops and Worcestershire sauce. Cook until scallops are done. Remove from heat. Season with salt and pepper. Mix in the cheese.

3. Place approximately 1 teaspoon of the scallop mixture in the centers of 30 of the bread circles.

4. Cover with the remaining bread circles. Seal the edges by pressing them together with the tines of a fork.

5. Heat the oil to between 350 and 360 degrees. Deep-fry the scallop sand dollars until golden brown. Serve hot.

Hot Salmon Tartlets

Yields 30 tartlets.

The mild blend of cream cheese, chives, almonds and olives brings out the best in salmon, the main ingredients in the filling for these crunchy bread tarts.

INGREDIENTS

1 cup canned salmon
½ cup cream cheese
3 tablespoons chopped chives
2 tablespoons chopped blanched
  almonds
2 teaspoons lemon juice
2 tablespoons chopped black olives
½ teaspoon garlic powder
30 Bread Tartlet Shells, page 104

INSTRUCTIONS

1. Combine well salmon, cream cheese, chives, almonds, lemon juice, olives and garlic powder.
2. Place tartlet shells on an ungreased baking sheet. Spoon a mound of filling into each bread shell.
3. Bake for 10 minutes at 350 degrees. Serve hot.

Shrimp Puffs

Yields 30 puffs.

A fluffy egg and cheese mixture blankets tender shrimp nestled on rounds of bread. In minutes, the individual rounds bake to heavenly golden puffs.

INGREDIENTS

½ cup butter, softened
1½ cups shredded sharp Cheddar
  cheese
1 egg, separated
15 4X4 sandwich slices white bread
30 cooked medium to small shrimp,
  shelled and deveined

SPECIAL EQUIPMENT
2-inch round cookie cutter

INSTRUCTIONS

1. Combine butter and cheese in a mixing bowl. Blend in the egg yolk.

2. Beat egg white until stiff. Fold into cheese mixture.

3. Cut each bread slice into two 2-inch rounds. Arrange the rounds on an ungreased baking sheet.

4. Top each round with a shrimp and cover with a rounded teaspoon of the cheese mixture.

5. Bake at 350 degrees for 15 to 18 minutes, or until golden brown.

SPECIAL HINTS
Bread rounds may be cut from white toast or any white, egg or rye bread.

Deep-Fried Shrimp Balls

Yields approximately 25 balls.

Taking its inspiration from the Orient, this recipe combines choice bits of fresh shrimp and water chestnuts to create mouth-watering morsels coated lightly with bread crumbs and gently deep-fried.

INGREDIENTS

1 pound raw shrimp, shelled, deveined
    and finely chopped
10 water chestnuts, finely chopped
½ teaspoon salt
½ teaspoon sugar
1 beaten egg
1 teaspoon soy sauce
¼ teaspoon ground ginger
1½ tablespoons cornstarch
¾ cup bread crumbs
Oil for deep frying

INSTRUCTIONS

1. In a mixing bowl, combine shrimp, water chestnuts, salt, sugar, egg, soy sauce, ginger and cornstarch. Mix thoroughly.
2. Shape the shrimp mixture into 1-inch balls and roll in bread crumbs.
3. Heat oil to 360 degrees, or until a drop of egg bubbles to the top.
4. Fry the shrimp balls until golden brown. Drain on paper towels.
5. Skewer with toothpicks and serve hot with Sweet Hot Mustard Sauce (see page 120).

Snapper Supreme Spread

Yields approximately 3 cups spread

Try this chilled fish spread with a zesty, full-bodied tomato flavor that keeps guests snapping back for more.

INGREDIENTS

1 pound red snapper fillets
3 tablespoons fresh lemon juice
Dash of salt and pepper
8-ounce can Italian tomato sauce
3 tablespoons chopped green pepper
6 pimiento-stuffed olives, chopped
1 tablespoon minced onion
1 tablespoon capers
2 tablespoons juice from the capers
2 bay leaves
¼ teaspoon garlic powder
¼ teaspoon marjoram
¼ teaspoon oregano
¼ teaspoon thyme
6 drops Tabasco sauce

INSTRUCTIONS

1. Cut the red snapper into bite-sized pieces. Place in a baking dish and sprinkle with lemon juice. Season with salt and pepper.
2. Place the remaining ingredients in a frying pan and simmer for 1 hour.
3. Pour seasoned tomato sauce on top of the fish. Bake in a 350 degree oven for 30 minutes.
4. Remove the bay leaves. Stir mixture until fish flakes and is thoroughly combined.
5. Cool, then refrigerate. Serve chilled in a lettuce-lined bowl accompanied by crackers or rye rounds.

DO-AHEAD NOTE

Snapper supreme can be made ahead of time and frozen.

Nine

Low Calorie, Health and Vegetable Hors d'Oeuvres

Whether you and your guests are interested in healthy, natural foods or are actively trying to lose weight, it's still possible to offer eye-appealing, taste-tempting hors d'oeuvres that will fit almost any diet. I've often wrestled with that one discouraging question: Why are the good things always so fattening? For all of us who have faced this problem, a portion of this chapter is specifically devoted to recipes that won't discourage calorie-conscious guests. And since each hors d'oeuvre is primarily composed of fresh vegetables and natural ingredient fillings, health food advocates can nibble contentedly, too.

Spices have been kept to a minimum in these hors d'oeuvres, since many special diets demand it. Fresh herbs can add zing to many dishes that otherwise call for spices, so use them freely.

The chapter is divided into three sections. The first group of recipes is specifically designed for low-calorie diets, while the second collection is oriented toward natural foods and includes such ingredients as whole wheat bread and sunflower seeds, which are slightly higher in calories. The third section is devoted to hot hors d'oeuvres of the vegetable variety. Many of these vegetables are nestled in tart shells or wrapped in pastry. While higher in calories, all contain healthy, fresh vegetables. Many of the recipes will suit both low-cal and natural food diets.

DO-AHEAD NOTE
Cold vegetable hors d'oeuvres are best when prepared the day of use. For hot vegetable hors d'oeuvres, see individual recipe suggestions.

Stuffed Cucumber Rounds

Yield may vary according to size of cucumbers used.

Colors, flavors and textures—this hors d'oeuvre has just the right combination of all of them.

INGREDIENTS

3 cucumbers
2 cans (7¾ ounces each) salmon
1 ounce cream cheese
1 teaspoon dried dill
Dash of garlic powder
½ cup finely diced red pepper

SPECIAL EQUIPMENT

Zester for scoring cucumbers

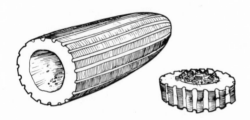

INSTRUCTIONS

1. Score the cucumbers with the zester. Slice approximately 1½ inches off one end and with a spoon, carefully hollow out the inside, removing the seeds, to form a tubular cucumber shell.
2. Prepare the filling by combining the salmon with the cream cheese, dill and garlic powder.
3. Fill the hollowed cucumbers with the salmon mixture and chill for 1 hour.
4. Just before serving time, carefully slice the scored cucumber into ½-inch rounds.
5. Garnish by lightly sprinkling each round with the diced red pepper for a colorful confetti effect.

SPECIAL HINTS

Reserve the leftover cucumber ends to use for Cucumber Daisies, below.

Cucumber Daisies

Yields 30 daisies.

Blooming with taste and texture, these daisy cups fashioned from the ends of cucumbers are as appetizing in flavor as they are low in calories! A gentle garnish of shredded carrots adds the final color contrast to this refreshing hors d'oeuvre.

INGREDIENTS

15 cucumbers
1 recipe Egg Salad, page 162, substituting low-fat mayonnaise for regular mayonnaise.
Small carrot, shredded

INSTRUCTIONS

1. Rinse the skin of the cucumbers thoroughly; peel if waxed. Cut a piece about 1½ inches long off each end of the cucumbers. Scoop out the center of each end piece to form cups.
2. With a sharp paring knife, scallop the edges of the cucumber cups to resemble daisy petals. Trim a thin slice of cucumber from the round end to give

the cucumber daisy a flat resting place.

3. Using a teaspoon, neatly fill each cucumber daisy to just below the carved petals with egg salad.

4. Sprinkle lightly with shredded carrot and refrigerate until serving time.

SPECIAL HINTS

Use the middle portion of the cucumber for Stuffed Cucumber Rounds, page 92.

Vegetable Kabobs

Yields 30 kabobs.

These colorful kabobs are hard to resist; luckily, even dieters won't have to try! Low-calorie and refreshing, the fresh vegetables get a zesty lift when served with a yogurt dip.

INGREDIENTS

30 Brussels sprouts
30 cherry tomatoes
2 large, firm avocados
Lemon juice
1 head red cabbage, hollowed out
    (optional, for presentation)
1½ cups plain low-fat yogurt
1 teaspoon garlic powder, or to taste

SPECIAL EQUIPMENT

Melon-baller
30 6-inch wooden skewers

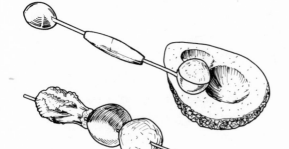

INSTRUCTIONS

1. Steam the Brussels sprouts just until tender and allow to cool.

2. Peel the avocados. Cut in half and remove the pit. Form balls with the large end of the melon-baller. Marinate each avocado ball in fresh lemon juice for 15 minutes.

3. On a wooden skewer, pierce an avocado ball, then a cherry tomato and finally a Brussels sprout.

4. Firmly secure each completed kabob porcupine-style in the hollowed cabbage or other base and refrigerate the whole creation until serving time.

5. Make a low-calorie dip by seasoning the yogurt with the garlic powder and refrigerate. Just before serving, fill the cabbage cavity with the chilled dip.

SPECIAL HINTS

Lemon juice adds a snappy flavor to the avocado, as well as prevents discoloration.

Accent each kabob with a carrot curl.

Tomato Accordions

Yields 30 accordions.

Italian tomatoes, because of their size and unusual shape, make beautiful little accordions. Filled with tempting tuna salad, this combination is healthy and low in calories.

INGREDIENTS

30 Italian plum tomatoes or 15 small tomatoes cut in half
1 recipe Tuna Salad, page 162, substituting low-fat mayonnaise for regular mayonnaise
¼ teaspoon garlic powder, or to taste
1 tablespoon chopped chives
Paprika

SPECIAL EQUIPMENT
Pastry bag (optional)

INSTRUCTIONS

1. Prepare the tomatoes by cutting out thin, V-shaped wedges with an extra-sharp paring knife across the length. Chill until time to fill.
2. Season tuna salad with garlic powder.
3. Fill each wedge of the chilled tomatoes with the tuna salad, using a teaspoon or a pastry bag without the tip.
4. Lightly sprinkle paprika on the filled accordions.
5. Chill until serving time.

SPECIAL HINTS

For an extra-low-calorie hors d'oeuvre, purchase tuna packed in water and mix it with low-fat mayonnaise.
Trim a thin slice off the bottom of each tomato to keep them stable.

Stuffed Brussels Sprouts

Yields 30 sprouts.

The beautiful little Brussels sprout becomes the pot and blossoms around a fluffy filling that looks and tastes sinfully rich, but isn't.

INGREDIENTS

30 Brussels sprouts
1 small cauliflower
1 to 2 tablespoons whole or skim milk
½ cup grated Parmesan cheese
2 tablespoons chopped chives
¼ cup sesame seeds

INSTRUCTIONS

1. Steam Brussels sprouts until tender.
2. Separate cauliflower into flowerets and steam until tender.
3. Whip the cooked cauliflower in a blender, adding just enough milk to moisten. Add the cheese and chives. Whip again in the blender and refrigerate.

SPECIAL EQUIPMENT
Sharp paring knife
Pastry bag without tip (optional)
Blender

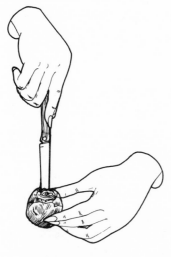

4. While the cauliflower mixture is cooling, cut and scoop out the centers of the Brussels sprouts. (Save the centers and toss them in tonight's salad.)

5. Fill the centers of the Brussels sprouts with the cauliflower-cheese mixture using a pastry bag without the tip, or a teaspoon.

6. Garnish lightly with sesame seeds and refrigerate until serving time.

Filled Artichoke Bottoms Greek-Style

Yields 25 to 30.

This hors d'oeuvre has the exotic elements and flavors of the Aegean. The artichoke bottom acts as a clever mini-platter for the luscious ingredients.

INGREDIENTS

12 ounces Feta cheese, crumbled
½ cup finely chopped pitted Greek olives
1 tablespoon low-fat mayonnaise
½ teaspoon summer savory
1 medium-sized firm tomato, finely chopped
4 jars (7 ounces each) marinated artichoke bottoms

INSTRUCTIONS

1. Prepare the filling by combining crumbled Feta cheese with chopped Greek olives, mayonnaise, savory and chopped tomato. Mix well and refrigerate for 1 hour.

2. Drain the artichoke bottoms and pat dry with a paper towel.

3. Spoon the cheese mixture generously onto the artichoke bottoms, smoothing it into a neat mound.

4. Refrigerate until serving time.

SPECIAL HINTS

The artichoke bottom is the meaty disclike portion found at the very bottom of the artichoke. Unlike artichoke hearts, bottoms have no leaves attached.

Filled Artichoke Hearts

Yields approximately 30 filled hearts.

Artichoke hearts are filled with a refreshing blend of spinach, onion and mayonnaise. Healthful, filling and easy on the calories!

INGREDIENTS

1 ½ cups cooked chopped spinach, well drained
2 tablespoons low-fat mayonnaise or imitation mayonnaise
¼ teaspoon garlic salt
3 tablespoons minced onion
6 jars (7 ounces each) marinated whole artichoke hearts
Pimiento strips (optional)

INSTRUCTIONS

1. To prepare the filling, combine the minced spinach with the mayonnaise, garlic salt and onion. Refrigerate for approximately one hour, so the flavors blend.
2. Drain the artichoke hearts and pat dry with a paper towel. Spread the leaves around the heart to make a small indentation in the center for the filling.
3. Spoon the spinach mixture onto the artichoke hearts and refrigerate until serving time.
4. Garnish with pimiento strips for additional color.

SPECIAL HINTS

Make sure to drain the minced spinach well. The consistency of this mixture should be thick. To thicken, add more spinach.

Tomato-Guacamole Cups

Yields 30 cups.

The colorful combination of refreshing avocado green and bright tomato red coupled with spicy flavor makes this hors d'oeuvre enticing anytime, but I especially recommend it for summer parties.

INGREDIENTS

30 cherry tomatoes
2 very ripe avocados, pitted and cubed
1 tablespoon low-fat sour cream
½ cup finely chopped onion
1 small package guacamole dip mix
1 teaspoon fresh lemon juice
Dash of cayenne pepper
Sunflower seeds

INSTRUCTIONS

1. Cut off tops of cherry tomatoes and reserve. Scoop out centers with a paring knife or small end of a melon-baller. (Save the tomato tops for garnishing). Chill the hollow tomatoes until time to fill.
2. To prepare the filling, whip the avocado and sour cream in a blender. Add the chopped onion, guacamole mix, lemon juice and cayenne pepper.
3. Pipe the mixture generously into the tomato

Holiday Hors d'Oeuvres. *Featuring assorted Barquettes, Canapés, and Hot Hors d'Oeuvres*

Dieter's Delight. *Featuring Vegetable Kabobs, Cucumber Daisies, and Stuffed Cucumber Rounds*

Tea Party. *Featuring assorted Tea Sandwiches and Canapés*

Elegant Noshes. *Featuring Chopped Liver Mold, Blintzes, and Lox Rollettes*

Ladies Club Luncheon. *Featuring Salmon Mousse and Tuna-Cucumber Mousse*

Candlelight Buffet. *Featuring Caviar and Egg Wedgewheel, Mini Fried Drumsticks, Iced Sandwich Torte, Anchovy-Cheese Squares, and assorted Barquettes, Tartlets, and Canapés*

Canapé Games. *Featuring Caviar and Cream Cheese Backgammon Set, Playing Cards, and Dominos*

Mini Meals. *Featuring hearty Smørrebrød Sandwiches*

From the Chafing Dish. *Featuring Tangy Fruit Riblets, Mini Fried Drumsticks, and Crepes*

Eggs Wonderful Eggs. *Featuring Pickled Pink Eggs, Shrimp Butterfly Eggs, Cameo Eggs, Caviar Grape Eggs, Stuffed Egg Cups, Egg Swans*

TV Picnic. *Featuring Cold Cut Platter, assorted Roll-Em-Ups and Toothpick Tidbits*

Champagne Buffet. *Featuring assorted Canapés, Tea Sandwiches, Barquettes and Tartlets, Liver Paté in Bread, Salmon Mousse*

cups using a pastry bag with a plain ½-inch tip, or a teaspoon.

4. Top with a sprinkle of sunflower seeds and cap with the tomato tops.

5. Refrigerate until serving time.

SPECIAL HINTS

Trim a paper-thin slice off the bottom of the tomatoes to keep them from rolling.

Whole Wheat-Avocado Triangles

Yields 32 triangles.

This hors d'oeuvre combines the rugged texture of healthful whole wheat muffins, the smoothness of avocado and the crunchiness of sunflower seeds—a naturally delicious concoction.

INGREDIENTS

1 medium-sized very ripe avocado
Italian seasoning to taste
½ clove garlic, crushed
6 or 7 cherry tomatoes
4 whole wheat English muffins
Sunflower seeds
½ cup alfalfa sprouts
½ cup grated Cheddar cheese

SPECIAL EQUIPMENT

Blender (optional)
Garlic press

INSTRUCTIONS

1. Mash the avocado in a blender or with a fork until it reaches a creamy smooth texture. Combine with Italian seasoning and garlic. Blend well.

2. Thinly slice the cherry tomatoes.

3. Toast the English muffins. Spread the avocado mixture smoothly on the muffin halves.

4. Sprinkle the sunflower seeds on the avocado spread. Add a thin layer of alfalfa sprouts and top with a light sprinkling of grated cheese. Refrigerate.

5. Just before serving, cut each muffin half into quarters, so that there are 4 triangles from each muffin half. Add a cherry tomato twist to each triangle as a garnish and serve.

Roquefort Mushrooms

Mushroom caps are stuffed with Roquefort cheese and sherry and conveniently broiled to produce a delicious bubbling hors d'oeuvre.

INGREDIENTS

30 medium to large mushrooms
4 ounces Roquefort cheese
1 cup garlic-flavored bread crumbs
¼ cup minced shallots
1 egg yolk
2 tablespoons dry sherry
¼ cup finely chopped fresh parsley

INSTRUCTIONS

1. Wash the mushrooms. Remove the stems. Set caps aside and mince the stems.
2. Prepare the filling by combining the Roquefort cheese, bread crumbs, minced mushroom stems, shallots and egg yolk. Mix thoroughly. Add the sherry and mix again.
3. Stuff each mushroom cap with a heaping mound of the Roquefort filling.
4. Place mushrooms under the broiler for 5 minutes. Garnish with chopped parsley and serve hot.

DO-AHEAD NOTE

Prepare and stuff the mushrooms in advance. Refrigerate until time to use. Broil and serve hot.

Cauliflower Boats

Delicately spiced and beautiful to behold, *bateaux de chou-fleur*, cauliflower boats, are an elegant hors d'oeuvre or a tempting side dish. The Emmenthal cheese adds just enough zip, yet doesn't overpower the subtle cauliflower.

INGREDIENTS

1 cup cauliflowerets
¼ cup heavy cream
½ cup shredded Emmenthal cheese
Pinch of white pepper
¼ teaspoon nutmeg
*1 recipe Barquette Pastry Shells
   dough, page 45*
Paprika

INSTRUCTIONS

1. Roll out dough to ¼-inch thickness and cut to fit 2½-inch-long boat-shaped molds. Fit dough into molds, weight with dried beans and bake in 475-degree oven for 8 to 10 minutes.
2. Steam the cauliflower until tender. Whip in a blender or mash.
3. Add the cream, cheese, white pepper and nutmeg. Mix thoroughly.

SPECIAL EQUIPMENT
Vegetable steamer (optional)
Blender or potato masher
2½-inch long boat-shaped tart molds

4. Fill the shells with the cauliflower-cheese mixture. Bake 10 minutes at 400 degrees. Garnish with paprika and serve hot.

DO-AHEAD NOTE
Prepare and bake the tart shells several days in advance. Freeze them in a moisture-proof container. Party time, fill and bake the tarts.

Carrot Tarts

Yields about 35 tarts.

Tasty and healthful, this recipe contains a unique combination of spices, fresh carrots, peanut butter and coconut, neatly packaged in a buttery tart shell. Though taboo for calorie counters, it's filled with protein and vitamin A.

INGREDIENTS

1 recipe Barquette Pastry Shells
   dough, page 45
1 cup cooked carrots
2 tablespoons peanut butter
½ teaspoon cinnamon
Pinch of nutmeg
Pinch of salt
¼ cup heavy cream
¼ cup shredded coconut

SPECIAL EQUIPMENT
2-inch round tart molds
Blender, food processor or potato
   masher
Electric mixer

INSTRUCTIONS

1. Roll out dough to ¼-inch thickness and cut to fit 2-inch round tart molds. Fit dough into molds, weight with beans and bake in 475 degree oven for 8 to 10 minutes.
2. Whip or mash the cooked carrots to a smooth consistency. Combine the carrots, peanut butter, cinnamon, nutmeg and salt. Mix thoroughly.
3. Whip the cream until stiff. Fold into the carrot-peanut butter mixture.
4. Spoon 1 teaspoon of the filling into each tart shell and bake at 400 degrees for 10 minutes.
5. Garnish with coconut and serve hot.

DO-AHEAD NOTE
Prepare and bake the tarts several days in advance. Freeze them, unfilled, in a moisture-proof container. Party time, fill and bake the tarts.

Stuffed Onions

Whether served as an hors d'oeuvre or as a side dish for a meal, these bite-sized stuffed onions, complete with cheese, capers and mushrooms, will please every vegetarian you know.

INGREDIENTS

30 small white boiling onions
½ cup butter
¼ cup chopped mushrooms
¾ cup shredded Gruyère cheese
½ tablespoon capers
1 egg yolk
½ cup bread crumbs
Salt and pepper to taste
1 tablespoon chopped pimiento

INSTRUCTIONS

1. Peel the onions and sauté in ½ cup butter over low heat for about 10 minutes, or until the onions are almost transparent. Remove onions with slotted spoon, reserving melted butter in pan, and drain on paper towels.

2. Slice about ¼ inch off the top of each onion. With a fork, remove a portion of the inside of the onion, leaving a round onion shell. Reserve the onion removed from the shell for other recipes.

3. Prepare the filling by combining 2 tablespoons of the reserved melted butter, the mushrooms, cheese, capers, egg yolk, bread crumbs and salt and pepper. Mix thoroughly and fill each onion shell with the mixture.

4. Bake 10 minutes at 400 degrees. Garnish with chopped pimiento and serve hot.

SPECIAL HINTS

Stuffed onions are best when prepared the day of use.

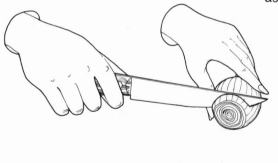

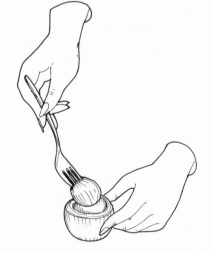

Fried Vegetable Kabobs

These sesame-sprinkled kabobs are a healthful treat for those who savor fruits and vegetables!

INGREDIENTS

30 plantain* slices, ¾ inch thick (about 3 bananas)

30 carrot slices, ¾ inch thick

1¾ cup flour

Pinch of baking soda

1 egg yolk

2 cups ice water

1 medium eggplant, cut into 30 1-inch cubes

1 bunch broccoli, cut into 30 flowerets

Sesame seeds

Vegetable oil for deep frying

Red cabbage (optional)

SPECIAL EQUIPMENT

30 6-inch bamboo skewers

Deep fryer

*If plantains, the large green bananas, are not available, you can substitute regular bananas that are not quite ripe yet. The taste is somewhat different but still pleasing.

INSTRUCTIONS

1. Prepare the batter by combining the flour, baking soda, egg yolk and ice water. Refrigerate until ready to use.

2. Skewer the vegetables and plantain on the bamboo sticks, putting an eggplant cube first, a plantain slice next, then broccoli and lastly the carrot.

3. Dip the kabobs into the chilled batter. Drain them slightly, then sprinkle on the sesame seeds.

4. Heat the oil to between 350 and 360 degrees.

5. Deep-fry the kabobs in the preheated oil until crisp and golden. Drain on paper towels and serve hot.

SPECIAL HINTS

If the plantains are to stand for any length of time, dip them in lemon juice to prevent them from turning brown.

DO-AHEAD NOTE

Prepare the batter and skewer the vegetables ahead of time. Refrigerate until ready to use. Party time, dip the skewers in the batter. Sprinkle with the sesame seeds, and deep fry.

SERVING SUGGESTIONS

Trim the bottom from a large red cabbage; plant the vegetable kabobs into the cabbage to create a porcupine effect. Or you can arrange the kabobs on a doily-lined serving tray. Place the ends of the skewers outward for your guests' convenience.

Samosa Crescents

Yields 25 crescents.

These crescents, overflowing with steamed vegetables and curry spices, are traditional Indian appetizers.

INGREDIENTS

4 tablespoons butter
2 cups sifted flour
2 egg yolks
6 tablespoons hot milk
Pinch of salt
2 tablespoons natural honey
2 tablespoons melted butter
1 teaspoon cinnamon
½ teaspoon curry powder
¼ teaspoon cumin
Pinch of thread saffron
½ cup chopped cooked broccoli
½ cup chopped cooked cauliflower
½ cup peas
¼ cup chopped walnuts
Oil for deep frying

SPECIAL EQUIPMENT

Medium-sized vegetable steamer
3-inch round cookie cutter
Deep fryer

INSTRUCTIONS

1. To prepare the pastry, cut the butter into the flour. Add the egg yolks, hot milk and salt. Knead lightly and form into a ball.
2. To prepare the filling, in a mixing bowl combine the honey with the melted butter, cinnamon, curry powder, cumin and saffron.
3. Add the cooked vegetables and nuts to the honey mixture and stir until the vegetables and nuts are completely coated.
4. Divide the dough in half and roll out each portion to a 14X7-inch rectangle. Cut into 3-inch rounds.
5. Fill one side of each round with a teaspoon of the vegetable mixture. Fold the dough in half to form a crescent. Lightly moisten the edges with water. Press them together with the tines of a fork both to seal and to decorate.
6. Heat oil to 360 degrees and deep-fry the samosa crescents until golden brown and crisp. Drain thoroughly on paper towels. Serve hot.

SPECIAL HINTS

Freshly steamed, still-firm vegetables are preferable for this recipe, but the frozen variety will work, too.

DO-AHEAD NOTE

Prepare the samosa crescents, fry them and freeze in a moisture-proof container. Before serving, heat the crescents in the oven for 10 minutes at 400 degrees.

Ten

❧ Hot Hors d'Oeuvres

❧ This chapter contains some piping-hot-straight-from-the-oven mini-versions of all-time favorites, such as miniature pizzas, hamburgers, quiches and soufflés—all neatly reduced to appetizing bite-sized hors d'oeuvre portions.

A variety of tasty ingredients, pastry wrappers and tarts combine to form additional favorites such as sausage blankets, ham cornucopias and barquettes. There is something for everyone and every taste, ranging from meats to cheeses—even tarts fashioned from bread, which contain a bubbling hot combination of the two, and sweet and sour won ton twists for those whose taste buds savor the Oriental influence.

Best of all, these hors d'oeuvres can be prepared, if not totally, at least partially in advance, then frozen, making preparation convenient and easily arranged to suit your schedule. On the day of your party, simply remove from the freezer as many as you want and continue with the preparations. Or, depending on the recipe, pop them in the oven when your guests arrive.

Tasty, imaginative hors d'oeuvres need no longer be passed-over for lack of time. These hors d'oeuvres are best when served hot, fresh out of the oven. They can be passed around on a serving tray or kept warm on an electric heating tray.

Sausage Bread Tartlets

Yields 30 tartlets.

There's something irresistible about the spicy aroma of pepperoni teamed with mozzarella cheese. Here the two favorites combine in a tasty hot meat tartlet. And that crunchy pastry is as easy as bread and butter.

INGREDIENTS

¾ cup ground pepperoni sausage
¾ cup shredded mozzarella cheese
1 egg, beaten
¼ cup minced onion
¼ cup minced green pepper
30 Bread Tartlet Shells (below)
¼ cup diced pimiento (optional)

SPECIAL EQUIPMENT

2-inch round tartlet molds

INSTRUCTIONS

1. Mix the ground sausage and the mozzarella. Add the egg, onion and green pepper, mixing thoroughly.
2. Fill each bread tartlet shell to the brim with the sausage-cheese mixture.
3. Bake at 400 degrees for 10 to 15 minutes, or until the cheese is melted. Serve hot, garnished with a tiny pimiento square if you wish.

Bread Tartlet Shells: [Yields 30 tartlet shells.] Cut 15 slices white bread in half. Press each half into a 2-inch round tartlet mold and trim off the excess by pressing the bread against the edge of the mold with your fingers. Melt ½ cup butter and brush generously on molded bread. Bake 10 minutes at 400 degrees. Cool, then unmold.

DO-AHEAD NOTE

Prepare, fill and bake the tartlets several days in advance. Freeze in a moisture-proof container. At party time, reheat the frozen tartlets in a 400-degree oven for 10 to 15 minutes, or until the cheese has melted. Serve hot.

Miniature Pizzas

Yields 40 miniature pizzas.

These miniature pizzas bubble over with a combination of two cheeses and other assorted savories. They're topped with a piquant anchovy for a touch of authenticity.

INGREDIENTS

2 tubes refrigerator dinner rolls
½ cup tomato paste
1 cup shredded mozzarella cheese
¼ cup minced onion
½ cup chopped pepperoni
½ cup minced green pepper
¼ cup diced mushrooms
1 tablespoon ground cumin seed
½ tablespoon oregano
½ tablespoon sweet basil
¼ cup grated Parmesan cheese
2-ounce can flat anchovy fillets,
*   chopped*

INSTRUCTIONS

1. Slice each refrigerator roll in half horizontally, forming two thin rounds, rather than one thick round. The rolls will lose their circular shape, so on a lightly floured surface, flatten each round slightly with a rolling pin and reshape the rolls into circles.

2. On each roll spread approximately ½ teaspoon tomato paste. Generously sprinkle with shredded mozzarella cheese.

3. Mix together onion, pepperoni, green pepper and mushrooms. Sprinkle on each roll.

4. Season with a dash of cumin seed, oregano, sweet basil, and a generous sprinkling of Parmesan cheese. Garnish with a tiny piece of anchovy.

4. Arrange the pizzas on an ungreased baking sheet and bake at 400 degrees for 15 to 20 minutes.

DO-AHEAD NOTE

Prepare and partially bake the ungarnished mini-pizzas for 5 to 8 minutes. Freeze in a single layer in a moisture-proof container. At party time, garnish and bake 10 to 15 minutes.

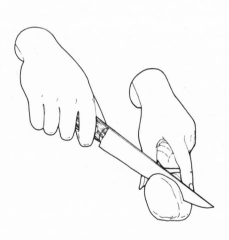

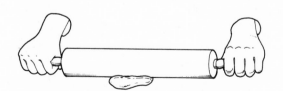

Sweet and Sour Won Ton Twists

Yields approximately 30 twists.

A touch of the Orient, these sweet and sour twists have the delectable crunch of fried won ton and the pungent flavor and aroma of the Far East.

INGREDIENTS

1 ½ tablespoons cornstarch
3 tablespoons red wine vinegar
½ cup water
½ teaspoon soy sauce
¼ teaspoon garlic powder
1 ½ tablespoons brown sugar
¼ teaspoon ground ginger
1 tablespoon catsup
Dash of salt and pepper
½ cup diced cooked pork
2 tablespoons diced onion
2 tablespoons diced green pepper
2 tablespoons chopped water
    chestnuts
2 tablespoons diced carrots
30 won ton skins
Oil for deep frying

SPECIAL EQUIPMENT
Deep fryer

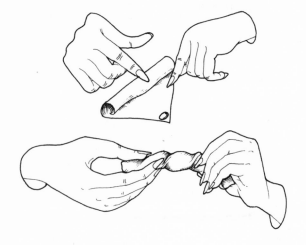

INSTRUCTIONS

1. To prepare the sweet and sour pork filling, dissolve the cornstarch in the wine vinegar and water and heat in a saucepan. Add the soy sauce, garlic powder, brown sugar, ginger, catsup, salt and pepper. Stir continuously over medium heat until the sauce becomes clear and thick. Add the pork, onion, green pepper, water chestnuts and carrots.
2. Cook the pork and vegetables over low heat for 5 to 7 minutes, stirring often. Remove from heat and allow the mixture to cool. It should be thick.
3. Separate the won ton skins and place them with one corner pointing toward you.
4. Place about ½ teaspoon of filling in the center of each skin. Roll up the skin, sealing the tip with a dot of water. Twist both ends to seal the filling.
5. In a deep fryer or deep heavy skillet, heat the oil to 360 degrees and deep-fry several twists at a time for approximately 1 minute, until the skins are golden brown and crisp.
6. Remove the twists from the oil and drain well on paper towels. Serve hot.

SPECIAL HINTS

During preparation, cover the unused won ton skins with a damp paper towel to keep them pliable.

DO-AHEAD NOTE

Prepare the sweet and sour won tons several days in advance. Fry them, then freeze in a moisture-proof container. At party time, heat the twists for 10 minutes at 400 degrees and serve hot.

Sausage Blankets

Ordinary cocktail hot dogs gain an air of elegant sophistication when wrapped in delicate sour cream pastry. The Gruyère cheese and chopped onion add zest to this attractive hors d'oeuvre.

INGREDIENTS

½ cup shredded Gruyère Cheese
½ cup minced onion
¼ teaspoon summer savory
Sour Cream Pastry (below)
30 cocktail hot dogs or your favorite
    sausage cut into 2-inch lengths
1 egg, beaten, for "egg wash"

INSTRUCTIONS

1. Prepare the filling by combining the cheese, onions and savory. Mix thoroughly.
2. Prepare the sour cream pastry according to the recipe below.
3. Knead the dough and divide it in half. Roll each half into a 7½X12½ -inch rectangle. Cut the dough into 2½-inch squares with a knife or pie fluter.
4. Place a teaspoon of the cheese-onion filling in the center. Place a cocktail hot dog diagonally in the center of each square, on top of the cheese filling. Wet diagonal corners with a drop of water and press together.
5. Arrange the blankets on a well greased baking sheet and brush them with the beaten egg.
6. Bake for 20 minutes at 350 degrees, or until golden brown.

Sour Cream Pastry: Combine 1 cup presifted flour, ½ teaspoon salt, ⅓ cup plus 1 tablespoon softened butter and ¼ cup sour cream. Knead lightly.

DO-AHEAD NOTE

Prepare the sausage blankets several days in advance and freeze them in a moisture-proof container. At party time, bake the blankets for 10 minutes at 350 degrees.

Shrimp Crescents

Chopped shrimp combined with cream cheese and dill weed provides an imaginative and tasty filling for this rich pastry crescent.

INGREDIENTS

1 recipe Sour Cream Pastry, page 107
1 cup chopped cooked shrimp
½ cup cream cheese, softened
¼ teaspoon dill
Pinch of tarragon
Pinch of salt
3 drops Tabasco sauce
1 egg, beaten

SPECIAL EQUIPMENT
3-inch round cookie cutter

INSTRUCTIONS

1. Prepare the shrimp filling by combining the shrimp, cream cheese, dill, tarragon, salt and Tabasco sauce in a mixing bowl. Set aside.
2. Prepare the dough. Roll out into two thin rectangles and cut into 3-inch rounds.
3. Place a spoonful of filling on half of each round. Fold over the other half to produce a half-moon effect. Press lightly with a fork to seal the edges.
4. Arrange the crescents on a well-greased baking sheet and brush each one with the beaten egg. Bake 10 to 15 minutes at 350 degrees.

Ham-Cheese Cornucopias

These tasty cornucopias are abundant with flavor. The richness of Boursin cheese and ham is enclosed in a delicious sour cream pastry wrapping.

INGREDIENTS

1 recipe Sour Cream Pastry, page 107
1 pound cooked ham, sliced ⅝-inch
   thick
½ cup Boursin cheese

SPECIAL EQUIPMENT
2½-inch round cookie cutter

INSTRUCTIONS

1. Prepare the sour cream dough and roll it out ¼ inch thick.
2. Cut the ham into sticks ⅝X1½ inches.
3. Spread the Boursin cheese lightly over the entire surface of the dough.
4. Cut 30 rounds of dough with the cookie cutter.
5. Place a ham stick in the center of each circle. Fold the bottom edges together and press lightly to form a cornucopia.
6. Bake on a well-greased baking sheet 15 to 20 minutes at 350 degrees.

Miniature Cannoli

Yields 30 cannoli.

Miniature cannoli are fashioned from refrigerator crescent rolls and filled with a creamy butter-cheese filling. Easy, elegant and sinfully rich!

INGREDIENTS

8-ounce tube refrigerator crescent rolls
6 ounces Brie cheese
¼ cup melted butter
¼ cup butter, softened at room
tempeature
1 tablespoon dry white wine

SPECIAL EQUIPMENT

Aluminum foil
Pastry bag with star tip

INSTRUCTIONS

1. Cut 30 3X12-inch rectangles out of heavy-duty aluminum foil. Fold the rectangles in half to 3X6 inches and roll into a tight cylinder ¾ inch in diameter. These foil cylinders will be the forms for the miniature cannoli and are reusable, so do save them.

2. Unroll the refrigerator dough and slice each triangle into several strips ½ inch wide.

3. Dip a dough strip in melted butter and spiral it around the foil. Begin and end about a ¼ inch from the top and bottom. Make sure the edges of the spiraling dough strips fit snuggly together.

4. Place the mini-cannoli on an ungreased baking sheet 2 inches apart. Bake as recommended for crescent rolls on the package.

5. While the cannoli are baking, combine the Brie, butter and wine. Whip until thoroughly blended. Place the mixture into a star-tipped pastry bag.

6. Allow the cannoli to cool, then push out the foil cylinder.

7. Pipe the cheese-butter mixture into each cannoli with the pastry bag and serve.

DO-AHEAD NOTE

Prepare the cannoli rolls several days in advance and freeze in a moisture-proof container. Warm slightly in the oven, then fill with the cheese-butter mixture. The filling is best when prepared the day of use.

Crab Barquettes

Boat-shaped tarts fashioned out of flaky pastry and brimming with a delicately seasoned seafood filling—delicious. And they're surprisingly easy to make.

INGREDIENTS

¾ cup crabmeat, flaked
4 ounces cream cheese, softened
1 teaspoon dill
1 teaspoon garlic powder
2 tablespoons dry white wine
30 prebaked Barquette Pastry Shells,
　page 45
Dash of paprika
Chopped chives

INSTRUCTIONS

1. Combine the flaked crabmeat with the cream cheese, dill, garlic powder and white wine. Mix thoroughly.
2. Spoon the filling generously into each baked barquette shell. Sprinkle with paprika.
3. Bake 5 to 7 minutes at 400 degrees, until heated through. Garnish with chives and serve hot.

DO-AHEAD NOTE

Prepare and freeze the filled barquettes several days in advance in a moisture-proof, airtight container. At party time, bake the barquettes 10 to 15 minutes at 400 degrees and serve hot.

Sherried Mushroom Croustades

White bread is brushed with melted butter, baked and cut to provide a crunchy showcase for your favorite savories.

INGREDIENTS

1 loaf unsliced white bread
½ cup melted butter
½ cup butter
½ pound mushrooms, coarsely
　chopped
2 tablespoons pale dry sherry
¼ cup chopped shallots
¼ cup grated Parmesan cheese

INSTRUCTIONS

1. To prepare the croustades, cut the bread horizontally into 4 slices about 1 inch thick.
2. Place the bread slices flat on a baking sheet and brush one side generously with melted butter.
3. Bake at 400 degrees for 10 to 12 minutes, or until golden brown and crisp.
4. Allow the bread to cool. Trim the crusts off and cut the slices into pattern #4.
5. To prepare the mushroom topping, melt ½ cup butter in a skillet. Add the mushrooms and shallots

and sauté over medium heat for 5 minutes. Add the sherry and cook for 5 minutes.

6. With a slotted spoon, remove the topping from the pan and generously cover the croustades.

7. Bake 10 minutes at 400 degrees and serve hot, garnished with a sprinkling of Parmesan cheese.

DO-AHEAD NOTE

Prepare the mushroom filling and the croustades several days in advance. Freeze them separately in moisture-proof containers. Before serving, thaw the filling, spoon it onto the croustades and bake 10 minutes at 400 degrees.

Miniature Hamburgers

Yields 32 mini-burgers.

The all-American favorite is transformed into bite-sized mini-burgers. The classic ingredients remain the same, but the preparation is simple and streamlined.

INGREDIENTS

2 cups freshly ground sirloin
1 egg yolk
½ cup minced onion
½ teaspoon ground pepper
Dash of hickory-smoked salt
¼ cup prepared mustard
1 tablespoon steak sauce
8 4X4-inch slices white bread, cut
  ½-inch thick
10 to 12 miniature sweet pickles, sliced
  into ½-inch discs

SPECIAL EQUIPMENT

1½-inch round cookie cutter

INSTRUCTIONS

1. In a mixing bowl, combine the ground sirloin, egg yolk, onion, pepper and hickory-smoked salt. Mix thoroughly.

2. Combine the mustard with the steak sauce. Spread lightly on the 8 bread slices.

3. Spread the ground sirloin mixture evenly on each bread slice in a layer about ½ inch thick.

4. With the cookie cutter, press 4 discs from each slice.

5. Garnish with a sweet pickle disc pressed into the center. Arrange the hamburgers on a baking sheet and bake 10 minutes at 375 degrees.

DO-AHEAD NOTE

Prepare the mini-burgers several days in advance and freeze them, unbaked, in a single layer in a moisture-proof container. Defrost and bake the hamburgers just before serving and serve hot.

Miniature Spinach Soufflés

Yields 30 miniature soufflés.

The elegance of a spinach soufflé is captured in a bite-sized hors d'oeuvre. The flaky pastry tart can be made days ahead and frozen, but you'll need some time just before your party to prepare the soufflé filling. The result is well worth the last minute preparation!

INGREDIENTS

1 recipe Barquette Pastry Shells dough, page 45
10-ounce package frozen chopped spinach, cooked and squeezed dry
1 tablespoon butter, softened
½ small onion, minced
2 tablespoons flour
½ cup milk
Dash of salt
Dash of pepper
½ teaspoon ground nutmeg
2 eggs plus 2 egg whites
1 tomato (optional)

SPECIAL EQUIPMENT

Tart shells, oblong or round, up to 3 inches

INSTRUCTIONS

1. Form pastry into tart shells using oblong or round molds up to 3 inches in diameter instead of boat-shaped molds. Bake as directed in recipe.
2. To prepare the soufflé filling, combine the spinach, butter, onion, flour, milk, salt, pepper and nutmeg in a medium saucepan. Mix thoroughly. Stir over moderate heat until the mixture begins to thicken. Remove the pan from the heat.
3. Separate the eggs and beat the yolks into the spinach mixture, one at a time. Transfer the mixture into a large bowl.
4. Beat all 4 egg whites until stiff. With a rubber spatula, carefully fold the egg whites into the spinach mixture.
5. Gently spoon the soufflé mixture into the pastry shells, filling to just below the brim.
6. Bake for 20 minutes at 400 degrees.
7. Garnish each tart with a strip of tomato, if you wish, and serve hot.

DO-AHEAD NOTE

Prepare the tart shells several days in advance. Freeze them in a moisture-proof, airtight container. Party time, prepare the soufflé mixture, fill the baked tart shells and bake.

Gruyère Cheese Balls

Crisp and golden on the outside, there's a surprise on the inside—smooth Gruyère cheese spiced with a hint of nutmeg.

INGREDIENTS

3 tablespoons butter
6 tablespoons flour
1 cup warm milk
½ teaspoon nutmeg
Freshly ground pepper and salt to taste
6 ounces Gruyère cheese, cubed
2 eggs, beaten
½ cup garlic-flavored bread crumbs
Oil for deep frying

INSTRUCTIONS

1. Melt the butter in a heavy enamel or stainless steel saucepan. Slowly blend in the flour and cook the mixture over low heat for 1 minute.
2. Add the milk all at once, along with the nutmeg and salt and pepper. Stir the mixture continuously with a wire whisk for approximately 10 minutes over low heat, until it thickens. Remove the pan from the heat and add the Gruyère cheese. Stir and allow the mixture to stand approximately 5 minutes.
3. When it is cool enough to handle, shape the slightly sticky mixture into small balls about 1½ inches in diameter.
4. Dip each cheese ball into the beaten eggs, then roll in bread crumbs until completely coated.
5. Heat the oil to 350 degrees.
6. Fry the cheese balls until golden brown and serve hot.

SPECIAL HINTS

If garlic-flavored bread crumbs are not available, add garlic powder to the plain variety.

DO-AHEAD NOTE

Prepare and fry the cheese balls several days in advance. Freeze them in a moisture-proof container. At party time, bake the cheese balls 10 minutes at 400 degrees.

Bacon Quiche Tartlets

Yields approximately 30 tartlets.

A great favorite—bacon quiche! This time the delicate French filling is nestled in miniature tart shells. Three different cheeses and a hint of Onion give this petite quiche extra zip.

INGREDIENTS

1 recipe Barquette Pastry Shells
   dough, page 45
1 cup heavy cream
4 ounces cream cheese, softened
2 eggs
½ teaspoon nutmeg
¼ teaspoon freshly ground pepper
Pinch of salt
1 cup shredded Swiss cheese
⅓ cup shredded Cheddar cheese
½ medium onion, minced
¾ cup crumbled cooked bacon

SPECIAL EQUIPMENT

2-inch round tart molds
Dried beans

INSTRUCTIONS

1. Form pastry into tart shells using 2-inch round molds. Fill with dried beans and bake at 475 degrees for 8 to 10 minutes. Remove beans and unmold.
2. Prepare the filling by combining the cream, cream cheese, eggs, nutmeg, pepper and salt in a blender or mixing bowl. Blend thoroughly.
3. Add the Swiss cheese, Cheddar cheese, onion, and crumbled bacon. Mix thoroughly.
4. Fill each tart shell to just below the brim and bake 15 to 20 minutes at 400 degrees.

DO-AHEAD NOTE

Several days in advance, prebake tart shells and freeze. At party time, fill with quiche mixture, and bake for 10 to 15 minutes at 400 degrees.

PHYLLO PASTRY HORS D'OEUVRES

These delicate paper-thin sheets of pastry are similar to strudel leaves. Lightly brushed with melted butter, they're filled, folded and baked.

A favorite at parties, phyllo pastry is rich, light and can be made with a wide variety of fillings, from meats and cheeses to seafood. Best of all, phyllo hors d'oeuvres can be made ahead of time and frozen. Phyllo dough may be purchased in Greek or Armenian delicatessens in one-pound packages. If frozen, the package may be defrosted overnight in the refrigerator. The paper-thin sheets tend to dry out quickly, so remove only a few sheets at a time. Reroll the rest and cover with a slightly dampened cloth.

DO-AHEAD NOTE

Filled phyllo hors d'oeuvres freeze well and can be stored approximately 1 month in a moisture-proof, airtight container.

Chicken-Cheese Phyllo Squares

Yields 30 squares.

INGREDIENTS

2 tablespoons butter
¼ cup minced onion
¼ cup minced mushrooms
1 cup minced cooked chicken
¼ cup shredded Swiss cheese
Dash of garlic powder
¼ teaspoon sweet basil
Dash of white pepper
1 egg, beaten
½ cup melted butter
1 package phyllo dough

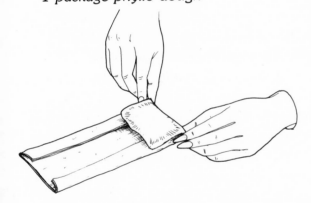

INSTRUCTIONS

1. Melt 2 tablespoons butter in a skillet. Add onion and mushrooms and sauté until onion is soft.
2. Combine sautéed onion and mushrooms with chicken, cheese, spices and beaten egg. Mix thoroughly.
3. Lightly brush 3 sheets of phyllo dough with melted butter and stack them one on top of the other. Cut the sheets lengthwise into 2½-inch strips.
4. Place 1 to 1½ teaspoons of filling on the bottom of each strip. Fold two sides of the strips in. Make a light crease ½ inch from the bottom and fold over to fashion a square. Seal the end with melted butter. Repeat with remaining phyllo dough and filling to form 30 squares.
5. Arrange the squares 2 inches apart on an ungreased baking sheet, seam side down. Bake at 375 degrees for 15 minutes or until golden brown.

Spinach-Cheese Phyllo Triangles

Yields 30 triangles.

INGREDIENTS

2 tablespoons butter
½ cup minced onion
1 tablespoon minced chives
10-ounce package frozen chopped spinach, defrosted and well drained
½ cup crumbled Feta cheese
1 egg, beaten
½ cup melted butter
1 package phyllo dough

INSTRUCTIONS

1. Melt 2 tablespoons butter in a skillet. Add onion and chives and sauté until onion is soft.
2. Combine sautéed onion and chives with the spinach, feta cheese and beaten egg. Mix thoroughly.
3. Lightly brush 3 sheets of phyllo dough with melted butter and stack them one on top of the other. Cut the sheets lengthwise into 2½-inch strips.

4. Place 1 to 1½ teaspoons of filling on the bottom of each strip. Fold one corner over to form a triangle and continue to fold corner to corner, flag fashion. Tuck the last fold under and seal with melted butter. Repeat with remaining phyllo dough and filling to form 30 triangles.

5. Place the triangles seam side down on an ungreased baking sheet 2 inches apart. Bake at 375 degrees for 15 minutes.

Crab Phyllo Rolls

Yields 30 rolls.

INGREDIENTS

2 tablespoons butter
¼ cup finely chopped onion
¼ cup finely chopped mushrooms
1 teaspoon dill
½ teaspoon Worchestershire sauce
1 teaspoon lemon juice
1 teaspoon flour
1 cup crabmeat, finely flaked
¼ cup chopped water chestnuts
½ cup melted butter
1 package phyllo dough

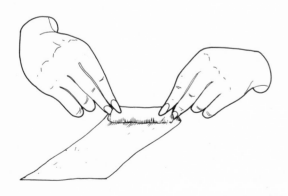

INSTRUCTIONS

1. Melt 2 tablespoons butter in a skillet. Add onion, mushrooms, dill, Worchestershire sauce and lemon juice. Sprinkle in flour and stir until all ingredients are well blended.

2. Add the crabmeat and water chestnuts. Stir again and cook 2 minutes more.

3. Lightly brush 3 sheets of phyllo dough with melted butter and stack them one on top of the other. Cut the sheets lengthwise into 2½-inch strips.

4. Place approximately 1 to 1½ teaspoons of filling at one end of each strip, ½ inch from the sides. Roll the dough and filling, tucking in the ends as you go along. Seal the ends with melted butter and place the rolls two inches apart, seam side down, on an ungreased baking sheet. Repeat with remaining phyllo sheets and filling to form 30 rolls.

5. Bake at 375 degrees for 15 minutes or until golden brown.

Eleven

🌿 From the Chafing Dish

🌿 Curiosity seems to get the better of us when it comes to appetizing aromas. At the first whiff of an appealing scent from the kitchen, we can't wait to see what's cooking. Hors d'oeuvres served in decorative chafing dishes, in particular, seem to hold a special attraction. As intriguing smells begin to permeate the room, party-goers always want to peek and see what's under the lids.

To help you satisfy their curiosity—and their appetites—this chapter offers some special twists on all-time chafing dish favorites and some out-of-the-ordinary recipes, too. They're perfect for the busy host or hostess because they can be prepared ahead of time and warmed up just before serving. Your guests will enjoy helping themselves, and you'll find they will have a great time gathering and conversing over the chafing dishes.

Some of the recipes feature luxurious cream or cheese sauces; others are served with tangy sauces that bring out the richness of the ingredients within. Whatever the variations, all of the chafing dish recipes have this in common: they're piping hot and full of flavor!

SERVING SUGGESTIONS
Provide plenty of toothpicks, cocktail napkins, small plates and forks where appropriate, for the convenience of your guests.

DO-AHEAD NOTE
All of these recipes can be prepared in advance and frozen in moisture-proof containers. Where indicated, the sauces are best frozen separately.

Cauliflower Clusters in Cheese Sauce

Yield will vary.

Delicate clusters of cauliflower are found in a rich sauce of cheese, cream and sauterne. This is especially for those who enjoy vegetables with the added tang of a creamy Cheddar cheese sauce.

INGREDIENTS

1 large head cauliflower
  (approximately 3 pounds)
½ cup butter
¼ cup chopped chives
16 ounces sharp Cheddar cheese, cut
  into small pieces
2 tablespoons flour
½ cup heavy cream
2 beaten egg yolks
3 tablespoons sauterne or sherry

INSTRUCTIONS

1. Cut the cauliflower into bite-sized florets.
2. In a frying pan, melt the butter. Add the cauliflower and the chives and cook, covered, for approximately 5 minutes. This is just to allow the flavors to blend; the cauliflower should not become too soft.
3. While the cauliflower is sautéing, prepare the sauce. Melt the cheese in a double boiler.
4. Mix the flour with the cream until smooth. Then add the egg yolks. Whisk the mixture into the melted cheese and stir frequently over low heat.
5. Add the sauterne and stir again.
6. Pour the cheese sauce into a chafing dish. Place the cauliflower clusters on top of the sauce. Skewer each cluster with a toothpick and serve.

Bacon-Wrapped Mushroom Caps

Yields 30 mushroom caps.

Mushroom caps wrapped in bacon strips are filled with a melt-in-your-mouth cheese mixture, then broiled to a tasty crispness.

INGREDIENTS

15 strips of bacon
30 small to medium mushrooms,
  stems removed
1 cup sharp spreadable Cheddar
  cheese
2 tablespoons minced onion
2 tablespoons bread crumbs
3 tablespoons sauterne

INSTRUCTIONS

1. Cut the bacon strips in half.
2. Wrap each bacon strip around the perimeter of each mushroom cap to create a small cuff. Fasten the bacon to the mushroom, catching both ends with a toothpick.
3. Broil the mushrooms 5 minutes, or until the bacon becomes slightly crisp.
4. Mix the cheese with the onion and bread

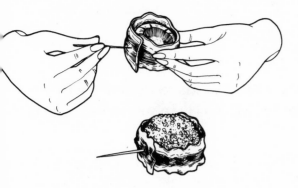

crumbs. Place a small mound of the cheese mixture inside each mushroom cap within the bacon cuff.

5. Broil for another 3 minutes. Transfer the mushrooms to a chafing dish containing the sauterne and serve hot.

Rumaki

Yields approximately 30 pieces.

Rumaki, the traditional chicken liver wrapped in bacon, gets a hint of the Orient when dashed with subtle pineapple-ginger sauce. Fast, easy, tasty.

INGREDIENTS

1¼ pounds chicken livers
½ cup butter
1½ teaspoons garlic powder
1½ teaspoons ginger
15 strips of bacon
16-ounce can pineapple chunks
    (reserve the juice)
2 tablespoons cornstarch
1 cup water
2 tablespoons brown sugar
1 teaspoon vinegar

INSTRUCTIONS

1. Sauté the whole chicken livers in butter, 1 teaspoon of the garlic powder and ½ teaspoon of the ginger until lightly brown.

2. Cut the livers into bite-sized pieces, approximately 1½ inches in diameter.

3. Cut the bacon strips in half. Roll a sautéed chicken liver piece in each bacon strip. Secure each roll with a toothpick and top with a pineapple chunk. Broil the rumaki until the bacon is crisp on both sides.

4. While the rumaki is broiling, prepare the pineapple-ginger sauce. Pour reserved pineapple juice into a sauce pan and dissolve cornstarch in the juice. Add the water, brown sugar, vinegar, remaining ½ teaspoon garlic powder and 1 teaspoon ginger. Heat the mixture until it becomes thick and clear. Pour into the chafing dish.

5. Place the broiled rumaki in the sauce in the chafing dish, with toothpicks angled up for easy service. Cover and serve hot.

Mini Fried Drumsticks

Yields 30 mini-drumsticks.

Guests rave about these mini-drumsticks, and they always wonder where you found such tiny chickens. Actually these irresistibles are made from chicken wings. Have plenty on hand—they go fast!

INGREDIENTS

30 chicken wings, wing tips removed
2 eggs, beaten
1 cup flour
1 teaspoon garlic powder
½ teaspoon pepper
¼ teaspoon salt
Oil for deep frying
Sweet Hot Mustard Sauce (below)
Plum Sauce (below)

INSTRUCTIONS

1. Push the meat from the thinner wing bone to one end and remove the small bone. This leaves one bone with all the meat surrounding it, resembling a drumstick.
2. Dip the mini-drumsticks into the beaten eggs and allow them to drain for a few minutes. Next dredge in flour seasoned with garlic powder, pepper and salt until they are fully coated.
3. Heat oil to between 350 and 360 degrees, or until a drop of beaten egg rises bubbling to the surface. Deep-fry several mini-drumsticks at a time until golden brown and crisp.
4. Place them, bone up, in a chafing dish. Serve hot with Sweet Hot Mustard Sauce and Plum Sauce.

Sweet Hot Mustard Sauce: Combine ½ cup dry mustard, ½ cup water and 2½ tablespoons sugar. Stir until smooth. Makes 1 cup.

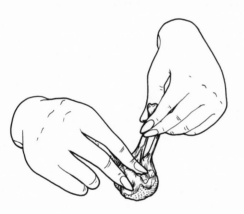

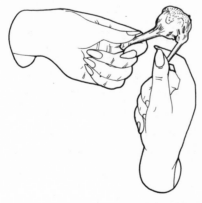

Plum Sauce: Combine ½ cup plum jelly, ¼ cup finely chopped chutney, ¼ cup catsup, 4 teaspoons vinegar and 2 teaspoons sugar in a saucepan. Simmer for 5 minutes. Makes 1 cup.

SPECIAL HINTS

Use wings from 2-pound chickens. If you order ahead, some butchers will reserve these for you.

Tangerine Chicken Cubes

Yields approximately 30 chicken cubes.

Succulent chicken breasts, trimmed into bite-sized cubes, complement the richness of this delicious, buttery orange sauce. A tangy tangerine section crowns each piece.

INGREDIENTS

1½ pounds boneless chicken breast
½ cup butter
½ teaspoon garlic powder
1 cup orange juice concentrate
 reconstituted with ½ cup water
2 tablespoons flour
Salt and pepper to taste
2 shakes of cinnamon
30 tangerine sections (canned or fresh)
2 tablespoons grated orange peel

INSTRUCTIONS

1. Cut the chicken breasts into 1½-inch cubes.
2. Melt the butter in a frying pan. Add the garlic powder and the chicken cubes. Sauté until the chicken is cooked.
3. Remove the chicken cubes from the frying pan with a slotted spoon.
4. Prepare the sauce by combining diluted orange juice and flour. Mix thoroughly. Add the orange juice mixture to the melted butter remaining in the frying pan. Stir and simmer until the sauce begins to thicken. Add salt, pepper and cinnamon.
5. Skewer a tangerine section and a chicken cube on each toothpick and place in a chafing dish. Pour the sauce over the skewered chicken. Sprinkle with grated orange peel and serve hot.

DO-AHEAD NOTE

Freeze the sauce and the chicken in separate containers. At part time, reheat; skewer the chicken cubes with tangerine sections just before serving.

Hickory-Flavored Mini-Dogs

Yields 60 mini-dogs.

These spicy cocktail hot dogs are perfect for large crowds. The zesty hickory-smoked flavor of the thick, rich sauce makes this a favorite.

INGREDIENTS

4 cups hickory-flavored barbecue
   sauce
2 cans (6 ounces each) prepared bean
   dip
1½ cups finely chopped onions
½ cup dark brown sugar
6 tablespoons dark molasses
¼ cup vinegar
1 teaspoon garlic powder
¼ teaspoon Tabasco sauce
¼ teaspoon salt (for extra hickory
   flavor use hickory-flavored salt)
¼ teaspoon pepper
60 cocktail hot dogs; regular size hot
   dogs may be cut into 1-inch
   mini-proportions as a substitute.

INSTRUCTIONS

1. In a large saucepan combine all the ingredients except the hot dogs. Simmer the mixture, for 10 to 15 minutes, stirring frequently. If the mixture becomes thicker than desired, thin out with a small amount of water, adding a tablespoon at a time. I prefer my sauce thick and hearty.
2. Add the mini-dogs to the sauce and simmer until they are warmed through.
3. Transfer the sauce and mini-dogs to a chafing dish and serve hot.

DO-AHEAD NOTE

Prepare the sauce several days in advance and refrigerate. At party time, add the mini-dogs to the sauce, heat thoroughly and serve.

Candied Mandarin Chicken Wings

Yields 30 chicken wings.

Miniature chicken wings are dipped in an egg batter, fried until golden brown, then baked in a tangy sauce that leaves them candy coated.

INGREDIENTS

30 chicken wings (wing tips removed)
2 eggs, well beaten
1 teaspoon garlic salt
¼ teaspoon pepper
Oil for deep frying
Sweet and Sour Sauce (below)
Sesame seeds

INSTRUCTIONS

1. Rinse chicken wings and dry thoroughly. Prepare the batter by combining, eggs, garlic salt and pepper.
2. Heat the oil to between 350 and 360 degrees, or until a drop of beaten egg rises to the top and bubbles. Dip the wings in the batter and fry several at a time until they are golden brown.

3. Drain the wings on paper towels and place them in a shallow baking dish.

4. Pour Sweet and Sour Sauce over the wings. Bake in a 350-degree oven about 30 minutes.

5. Transfer wings and sauce into a chafing dish, sprinkle with sesame seeds and serve hot.

Sweet and Sour Sauce: In a saucepan combine 1 cup brown sugar, 1 cup vinegar, ½ cup water, ½ cup pineapple juice, ¼ cup catsup, 1 tablespoon soy sauce and ½ teaspoon salt. Bring to a boil.

SPECIAL HINT

This recipe is best made with the wings from 2-pound chickens. If you order ahead, some butchers will reserve these for you.

Hot, Saucy Swedish Meatballs

Yield will vary.

A hearty dish that is simple to prepare and always proves a crowd pleaser. Swedish meatballs are sautéed in butter, then gently simmered in a thick, spicy beef bouillon sauce.

INGREDIENTS

4 4X4 sandwich slices white bread
¼ cup cream
1½ pounds ground round
1 tablespoon minced onion
½ teaspoon salt
2 eggs, slightly beaten
5 tablespoons butter
3 tablespoons flour
2 cups beef bouillon
½ teaspoon Tabasco sauce
1 tablespoon dry mustard
1 tablespoon white horseradish
¼ teaspoon celery salt

INSTRUCTIONS

1. Trim crusts from the bread and soak slices in cream for approximately 4 minutes.

2. Mix the softened bread with the ground round, onion, salt, and eggs. Form into 1-inch balls.

3. Melt the butter in a skillet and sauté the meatballs until they are brown. Reserve pan drippings.

4. To prepare the sauce, combine the flour with the beef bouillon in a large saucepan. Bring the mixture to a boil, stirring constantly, until smooth.

5. Add the Tabasco, mustard, horseradish and celery salt; stir. Add the meatballs with pan drippings to the sauce. Simmer gently for 3 minutes.

6. Transfer the meatballs and sauce to a chafing dish and serve hot.

Tangy Fruit Riblets

Yields 40 to 50 riblets.

Shades of Polynesia! These sweet and sour mini-ribs are exotically delicious. A tangy sauce loaded with pineapple, blueberries and walnuts makes this hors d'oeuvre "finger-lickin' good."

INGREDIENTS

2 to 3 pounds spareribs (cut into strips
   of 1½ to 2 inches long,) for
   approximately 40 to 50 riblets*
½ cup lemon juice
16-ounce can pineapple chunks
   (reserve the juice)
½ cup water
2½ tablespoons cornstarch
1 cup orange marmalade
¼ cup vinegar
2 tablespoons catsup
1 teaspoon garlic powder
1 teaspoon soy sauce
½ cup blueberries—frozen, canned, or
   fresh
¼ cup chopped walnuts

* Ask your butcher to do this for you.

INSTRUCTIONS

1. Brush ribs with lemon juice and bake 1 to 1½ hours at 350 degrees, until pork is thoroughly cooked. Baste frequently with lemon juice.
2. To prepare the tangy fruit sauce, combine the reserved pineapple juice and water in a medium saucepan and dissolve cornstarch in the liquid. Add marmalade, vinegar, catsup, garlic powder and soy sauce.
3. Heat, stirring the mixture frequently until it becomes thick and clear.
4. Add the pineapple chunks, blueberries and chopped walnuts.
5. Cut the strips of baked ribs into individual bite-sized riblets. Stir them into the sauce until the riblets are completely coated.
6. Transfer the mixture to a chafing dish and serve hot.

Cherry-Raisin Pork Cubes

Yield will vary.

In the grand tradition of the pork roast in cherry sauce, this hot hors d'oeuvre makes an elegant offering at your feast table. Sesame seeds add a crunchy contrast to the spiced cherry and raisin sauce.

INGREDIENTS

*1½ pounds boneless pork loin roast
  (rib end)*
21-ounce can cherry pie filling
1 tablespoon vinegar
½ cup golden raisins
½ cup chopped onion
½ teaspoon ground cloves
¼ teaspoon garlic powder
¼ teaspoon ground pepper
*2 cups green pepper cut into 1-inch
  chunks*
¼ cup sesame seeds

INSTRUCTIONS

1. Roast the pork using your favorite method. When cool, cut the meat into 1-inch cubes.
2. To prepare the sauce, combine pie filling, vinegar, raisins, onion, cloves, garlic powder and pepper. Heat the sauce to a gentle boil, then reduce to a simmer.
3. Add the green pepper and pork cubes. Simmer gently 10 more minutes.
4. Transfer the mixture to a chafing dish, sprinkle on sesame seeds and serve hot.

SPECIAL HINTS

Skewer the pork cubes and green peppers with toothpicks for convenient self-service. Keep covered and serve hot.

Twelve

❧ Miniature Crepes

❧ Theme your next gathering "Candelight and Crepes." What could be more elegant? Crepes lend that special air of sophistication and grace to any party. Miniature crepes are particularly appropriate because they are just the right size for an infinite number of hors d'oeuvres. Use the wafer-thin wrappers to envelop an assortment of the delectable fillings in this chapter; then watch as your guests sample with delight. Soon enough, they'll be asking for your recipes!

Serve your crepes in a chafing dish to keep them hot and tasty. Top them with splendid sauces that enhance the flavors of the surprise fillings. The sauces can be served in gravy boats or containers, which can be kept warm and placed alongside the crepes. These separate serving dishes will keep your crepes firm and avoid sogginess.

With these tips in mind, start planning your party! Light yet filling, the mini-crepes will keep your guests delightfully satisfied and eagerly conversing until the candles burn low.

DO-AHEAD NOTE

Fillings, like the crepes, may be prepared beforehand and frozen. At party time, just thaw, fill and fold. Place the crepes in a chafing dish to keep them warm, or heat them in the oven, preferably in an oven-to-table platter from which they can be transferred to small serving plates.

I have discovered the sauces are best when fresh—either made early on the day they are served, then refrigerated and reheated, or made just before serving time. Sauces yield 2 cups each.

SPECIAL HINTS

Instructions for folding and rolling crepes are found on page 128.

SERVING SUGGESTIONS

Place the crepes on small plates and ladle the sauce generously over the individual servings.

Miniature Hors d'Oeuvre Crepes

The elegant crepe is at its best when it is light, tender and very thin. Though this sounds like a difficult task, it is not, and the key, of course, is in the batter. These easy French pancakes can be made ahead of time and frozen for later use. They make a tasty wrapper for any of the luscious fillings described on the next few pages.

INGREDIENTS

3 eggs, lightly beaten
1½ cups milk
1¼ cups presifted flour
Dash of salt
Butter

SPECIAL EQUIPMENT

5-inch frying pan or crepe maker

INSTRUCTIONS

1. To prepare the crepe batter, beat the eggs until light and foamy. Add the milk. Slowly add the flour and salt for a smooth, creamy batter. This may be quickly done in a blender. Refrigerate batter for an hour, if you have time.
2. Heat a 5-inch frying pan until a drop of water beads and rolls around. Spread a thin film of butter on the surface. This may be done with a paper towel, but a light hand is the key here. Repeat this step after each crepe.
3. Pour 2 tablespoons of batter into the center of the pan. Tilt the pan quickly so that batter spreads evenly leaving a wafer-thin crepe.
4. When one side is lightly brown, turn the crepe out onto a plate.

SPECIAL HINTS

Whenever possible allow the batter to chill in the refrigerator approximately 1 hour before using. This makes for a lighter, more tender crepe.
When adding the batter to the pan, take the pan temporarily off the heat.

DO-AHEAD NOTE

Crepes may be made ahead of time and frozen by stacking them with wax paper between each layer. Place the stack into a moisture-proof container and freeze flat. This way you can use as many as you need and keep the rest frozen.

Mini Lobster Newberg Crepes

For those who love elegance, the *pièce de resistance*. This crepe combines the richness of lobster with the sophistication of a mild cognac sauce.

INGREDIENTS

¼ cup butter
1 teaspoon minced chives
½ teaspoon chopped dill
2 tablespoons Madeira wine
2 cups chopped cooked lobster
25 Miniature Hors d'Oeuvre Crepes,
  page 127
Cognac Sauce (below)

INSTRUCTIONS

1. Melt ¼ cup of the butter in a skillet over medium heat. Add the chopped dill weed, Madeira and lobster. Sauté 3 to 5 minutes.
2. Place 1 tablespoon of the filling in the center of each crepe.
3. Fold two sides over the filling and roll the crepe tightly. Place the crepes in the chafing dish and cover tightly to keep warm. Serve with cognac sauce.

Cognac Sauce: To prepare the sauce, melt ¼ cup butter in a saucepan. Gradually blend in 4 tablespoons flour and salt to taste. Cook, stirring, over medium heat for 2 to 3 minutes. Whisk in 2 cups milk and cook over moderate heat, stirring constantly, until the mixture thickens. Add ¼ teaspoon dill and 2 tablespoons cognac. Stir over low heat for 2 minutes. Taste for seasoning. Transfer the sauce to a separate container. Serve hot.

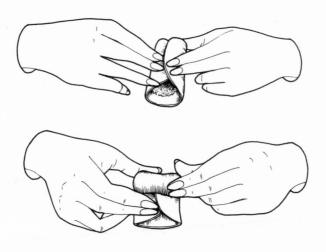

Hot Spinach Crepes

Spinach is combined with anchovies, onions and egg to make this tasty filling. Then topped with a rich cream cheese-sherry sauce.

INGREDIENTS

2 cups frozen chopped spinach
2 tablespoons butter
2 tablespoons diced onion
2 tablespoons chopped anchovies
1 egg, beaten
25 Miniature Hors d'Oeuvre Crepes,
  page 127
Cream Cheese-Sherry Sauce (below)

INSTRUCTIONS

1. Cook the spinach according to the directions on the package. Drain thoroughly.
2. Melt 2 tablespoons of the butter in a skillet. Add the onion, anchovies and spinach; stir. Add the beaten egg and cook for 3 minutes over medium heat, stirring until all ingredients are mixed and egg is completely absorbed.
3. Fill each crepe with 1 tablespoon of filling. Fold 2 sides over the filling and roll the crepe tightly. Place the rolled crepes in a chafing dish and cover tightly to keep them warm. Serve with cream cheese-sherry sauce.

Cream Cheese-Sherry Sauce: To prepare the sauce, melt ⅓ cup butter in a saucepan. Gradually stir in 5 tablespoons flour. Cook, stirring, over medium heat for 2 to 3 minutes. Beat in 1½ cups milk. Continue stirring until the sauce thickens. Add a dash of salt, ¼ cup pale dry sherry, ½ teaspoon dill and 2 ounces softened cream cheese. Stir over low heat until sauce is smooth. Transfer the sauce to a separate container and serve hot alongside the crepes.

Sherried Mushroom Crepes

With ingredients like mushrooms, onions, sherry, cream and Cheddar cheese, it is hard to go wrong. Here they are fashioned into a rich and sumptuous crepe that party-goers will take an instant liking to.

INGREDIENTS

¼ cup butter
¼ cup chopped onion
1 bouillon cube
2 tablespoons dry sherry
2 cups sliced small mushrooms
25 Miniature Hors d'Oeuvre Crepes,
    page 127
Cheddar Cheese-Sherry Sauce (below)

INSTRUCTIONS

1. Melt butter in a skillet. Add the onion, bouillon cube, sherry and mushrooms. Simmer over medium heat 3 to 5 minutes.
2. Fill each crepe with 1 tablespoon of the filling. Fold two sides in over the filling and roll tightly. Place the crepes in a chafing dish and cover tightly to keep warm. Serve with Cheddar cheese-sherry sauce.

Cheddar Cheese-Sherry Sauce: To prepare the sauce, melt 1½ cups grated Cheddar cheese in a double boiler. Add ¼ cup cream, 1 teaspoon sherry and a dash of white pepper and mix thoroughly. Transfer the Cheddar cheese sauce to a separate serving container that can be kept warm and place it alongside the crepes.

SPECIAL HINTS

The Cheddar-sherry sauce is especially tasty when prepared just before serving.

Mini Sausage 'n' Apple Crepes

Yields 25 crepes.

Hot applesauce is a sweet companion to this sausage and apple treat. Don't skimp on the cinnamon; it enhances the flavor of both the sausage and the apples.

INGREDIENTS

1 ½ cups diced spicy Polish sausage
½ cup diced apple
⅛ teaspoon cinnamon
Dash of pepper
25 Miniature Hors d'Oeuvre Crepes, page 127
Hot Applesauce (below)

INSTRUCTIONS

1. Brown the sausage in a skillet.
2. Add the apple and cook over medium heat just until the apples start to soften. Drain any excess liquid and stir in the cinnamon and pepper.
3. Place 1 tablespoon of the sausage-apple filling in the center of each crepe. Fold in two sides of the crepe over the filling and roll up tightly. Keep warm in chafing dish. Serve with hot applesauce.

Hot Applesauce: To prepare the sauce, heat 2 cups applesauce. Add a dash of cinnamon and transfer into a separate serving container. Serve hot.

Crispy Crepes

Yields 25 crepes.

These creamy cheese-filled crepes are sinfully rich, but once your guests sample them, they will find it difficult not to indulge. Dipped in egg and rolled in bread crumbs, they are deep-fried until deliciously crisp.

INGREDIENTS

1 cup grated Swiss cheese
1 cup butter, softened
½ teaspoon nutmeg
2 teaspoons pale dry sherry
25 Miniature Hors d'Oeuvre Crepes, page 127
2 eggs, lightly beaten
½ cup bread crumbs
Oil for deep frying

INSTRUCTIONS

1. In a mixing bowl, combine the cheese and softened butter. Stir in the nutmeg and sherry. Mix until all ingredients are thoroughly blended.
2. Place a tablespoon of the mixture in the center of each crepe. Fold two sides in over the filling and roll tightly.
3. Dip the rolled crepes in the beaten eggs. Drain slightly, then coat in bread crumbs.
4. Heat oil to 360 degrees. Deep-fry the crepes until golden. Drain on paper towels and serve hot.

Bacon, Tomato and Cheese Crepes

Yields 25 crepes.

Here's a dish even the kids will enjoy! Bacon, tomato, green pepper, onions and cheese create a creamy, crunchy filling for crepes, which are topped with a splendid Cheddar cheese sauce.

INGREDIENTS

⅓ cup butter
2 tablespoons minced onion
½ cup diced green pepper
¾ cup crumbled cooked bacon
½ cup diced tomato
½ cup shredded Cheddar cheese
Dash of pepper
25 Miniature Hors d'Oeuvre Crepes, page 127
Cheddar Cheese Sauce (below)

INSTRUCTIONS

1. Melt butter in a skillet. Add the onion and green pepper and sauté until onion is soft. Next add the bacon, tomato, cheese and pepper. Sauté just until the cheese begins to melt.
2. Fill each crepe with 1 rounded tablespoon of the filling. Fold two sides in over the filling and roll tightly. Place the rolled crepes in a chafing dish and cover tightly to keep warm. Serve with Cheddar cheese sauce.

Cheddar Cheese Sauce: To prepare the sauce, melt ¼ cup butter in a saucepan. Gradually stir in ¼ cup flour. Cook, stirring, for a few minutes to make a roux. Add dash of salt and 1 cup milk. Continue to cook, stirring, until the sauce thickens. Add ¾ cup grated Cheddar cheese. Stir over low heat until the sauce is smooth. Transfer the sauce to a separate container and serve hot alongside the crepes.

Chicken Liver Crepes Vermouth

Yields 25 crepes.

Chicken livers are sautéed in butter and vermouth and subtly accented with the garden's herbal offerings: shallots, basil and thyme. A light cream sauce is the final, delectable flourish.

INGREDIENTS

2 tablespoons butter
½ cup chopped shallots
1 tablespoon dry vermouth

INSTRUCTIONS

1. Melt ¼ cup of the butter in a skillet. Add the shallots, vermouth, basil and thyme. Add the chicken livers, and sauté until cooked through.

1 teaspoon sweet basil
½ teaspoon thyme
2 cups (about 1 pound) chicken livers
   trimmed and diced
25 Miniature Hors d'Oeuvre Crepes,
   page 127
Cream Sauce (below)

2. Place 1 tablespoon of the chicken liver filling in the center of each crepe. Fold two sides in over the filling and roll the crepe tightly.

3. Place the rolled crepes in the chafing dish and cover to keep warm. Serve with cream sauce.

Cream Sauce: To prepare the sauce, melt 2 tablespoons butter in a saucepan. Add 1 tablespoon chopped chives. Add 3 tablespoons flour and cook over moderate heat, stirring, for a few minutes to make a roux. Whisk in 1½ cups milk gradually. Cook, stirring, until mixture thickens. Beat with a whisk until smooth. Combine 3 egg yolks with ½ cup heavy cream. Whisk into the milk and flour mixture. Pour the cream sauce into a separate container. Serve hot.

Mini Ham 'n' Cheese Crepes

Yields 25 crepes.

Those old favorites, ham and Swiss cheese, are teamed again, but this time they get a snappy lift from a fruity pineapple sauce served with this unique mini-crepe.

INGREDIENTS
1½ cups diced cooked ham
¾ cup shredded Swiss cheese
1 teaspoon rosemary
25 Miniature Hors d'Oeuvre Crepes,
   page 127
Pineapple Sauce (below)

INSTRUCTIONS
1. Combine ham and cheese in a mixing bowl. Add the rosemary. Blend thoroughly.
2. Place 1 tablespoon of the ham and cheese mixture in the center of each crepe. Fold two sides over the filling and roll the crepe tightly.
3. Place the crepes in the chafing dish and cover tightly. The cheese will melt into the ham while in the chafing dish. Serve with pineapple sauce.

Pineapple Sauce: To prepare the sauce, combine 1 cup pineapple juice and ½ cup water in a saucepan. Dissolve 2 tablespoons cornstarch in the liquid. Add a dash of cloves and cinnamon and simmer until the mixture becomes thick and clear. Add 1 cup crushed pineapple and mix thoroughly. Transfer the hot sauce to a separate container. Serve hot.

Mini Shrimp Crepes

Yields 25 crepes.

Tiny shrimp sautéed with shallots and a delicate blend of seasonings create crepes that will be remembered long after they are gone. Top them with a hot green goddess sauce for added richness and flavor.

INGREDIENTS

¼ cup butter
1 tablespoon minced shallots
½ teaspoon sweet basil
2 tablespoons lemon juice
2 tablespoons chopped celery
¼ teaspoon garlic powder
¼ teaspoon dill
2 cups tiny cooked shrimp
Green Goddess Sauce (below)
25 Miniature Hors d'Oeuvres Crepes,
    page 127

INSTRUCTIONS

1. Melt the butter in a frying pan. Add the shallots, basil, lemon juice, celery, garlic powder, dill and shrimp. Sauté for 3 minutes over medium heat.
2. Spoon 1 tablespoon of shrimp filling into the center of each crepe. Fold in two sides of the crepe over the filling and roll up tightly.
3. Place the mini-crepes in a chafing dish, cover tightly to keep them warm. Serve with green goddess sauce.

Green Goddess Sauce: To prepare the sauce, melt ⅓ cup butter in a saucepan. Gradually stir in ¼ cup flour. Cook, stirring, over medium heat for 2 to 3 minutes. Beat in 1½ cups milk and cook, stirring, until the sauce thickens. Add 2 tablespoons green goddess dip mix. Stir over low heat until sauce is smooth. Season to taste with salt and pepper. Transfer the sauce to a separate container and serve hot alongside the crepes.

Ratatouille Crepes

What to serve your vegetarian friends? A healthy, vitamin-wealthy crepe whose vegetables are sautéed, then simmered. Topped with a hot melted Swiss cheese sauce, the crepe is irresistible.

INGREDIENTS

¼ cup butter
Salt and pepper to taste
½ teaspoon garlic powder
½ teaspoon sweet basil
Dash of Tabasco sauce
½ cup diced zucchini
½ cup diced peeled eggplant
½ cup diced onion
½ cup diced tomatoes
½ cup diced green pepper
25 Miniature Hors d'Oeuvre Crepes, page 127
Swiss Cheese Sauce (below)

INSTRUCTIONS

1. Melt the butter in a medium-sized saucepan. Add the salt, pepper, garlic powder, basil and Tabasco. Blend thoroughly.
2. Add the diced zucchini, eggplant, onions, tomatoes and green pepper. Mix thoroughly. Cover and allow the mixture to simmer until the vegetables are tender but not too soft.
3. Fill each crepe with approximately 1 tablespoon of the ratatouille mixture. Fold 2 sides in over the filling and roll tightly. Transfer the crepes into a chafing dish and cover tightly to keep warm. Serve with Swiss cheese sauce.

Swiss Cheese Sauce: To prepare the sauce, melt ¼ cup butter in a saucepan. Gradually stir in ¼ cup flour. Continue stirring over medium heat for 2 to 3 minutes. Beat in 1½ cups milk and cook, stirring, until the sauce thickens. Add the salt to taste and ½ cup grated Swiss cheese and stir over low heat until sauce is smooth. Transfer the sauce to a separate container and serve hot alongside the crepes.

Chicken-Date Crepes

Yields 25 crepes.

This mini-crepe filling combines chicken, almonds and spices with a sweet surprise—chopped dates. A hot, sherried mushroom sauce adds a rich, thick complement.

INGREDIENTS

¼ cup butter
1½ cups diced cooked chicken
2 tablespoons chopped chives
½ teaspoon garlic powder
Pepper to taste
2 tablespoons chopped almonds
¼ cup chopped dates
25 Miniature Hors d'Oeuvre Crepes, page 127
Sherried Mushroom Sauce (below)

INSTRUCTIONS

1. Melt the butter in a skillet. Add the chicken, chives, garlic powder and pepper. Sauté the chicken until tender.
2. Add the almonds and dates and mix thoroughly.
3. Place approximately 1 tablespoon of the filling in the center of each crepe. Fold two sides over the filling and roll the crepe tightly. Place the crepes in the chafing dish and cover tightly to keep them hot. Serve with sherried mushroom sauce.

Sherried Mushroom Sauce: To prepare the sauce, combine a 10¾-ounce of undiluted cream of mushroom soup and ½ cup cream in a saucepan. Heat and stir the mixture until it is thoroughly blended. Add ¼ cup pale dry sherry and simmer 2 minutes to blend flavors. Pour the mushroom sauce into a separate container and serve hot.

Thirteen

🌿 Tortes, Pies and Hors d'Oeuvre Games

🌿 Tortes, pies and games are featured in this distinctive collection of hors d'oeuvres. Pastrys, breads, fillings and a rainbow of vegetables combine to form unique patterns and geometric designs. Unusual hors d'oeuvre pies are fashioned from a layer of flaky pie crust followed by a piquant spread and topped with a colorful arrangement of garnishes. Showstoppers such as elegant Iced Sandwich Torte, Confetti Cheese Wheel and Caviar Cheese Pie are found in this chapter.

For an added touch of whimsey, an edible backgammon game is included, which can be assembled quickly from cream cheese and caviar. While results of these pies and games are spectacular, the fun (aside from the eating) is in the preparation. For assembling some of them is much like working a puzzle of the most delectable variety.

DO-AHEAD NOTE

Tortes, pies and games can all be assembled several hours before serving for convenience. Pie crusts, spreads and garnishes can be prepared the day before and stored separately.

Iced Sandwich Torte

Yields 10 to 12 wedges.

Chicken, ham and egg salads form the fillings between three layers of white bread. This grand sandwich is then frosted with a mixture of cream cheese and mustard. Topped with a tomato rose and served chilled, it's delightful.

INGREDIENTS

Round loaf white bread, 7 to 9 inches round, unsliced
½ recipe (approximately 1½ cups) Pineapple-Chicken Salad, page 161
½ recipe (1 cup) Ham Salad, page 162
½ recipe (1 cup) Egg Salad, page 162
¼ cup butter, softened
20 ounces cream cheese, softened
2½ tablespoons prepared mustard

SPECIAL EQUIPMENT
Pastry bag with star tip

INSTRUCTIONS

1. Trim the crust from around the top and bottom of the bread, leaving a smooth surface.
2. Cut the bread horizontally into 3 equal layers. Spread each layer with butter and one of the fillings. Stack the layers and refrigerate.
3. To prepare the icing, combine 16 ounces of the cream cheese and the mustard. Blend thoroughly. Frost the sandwich torte evenly.
4. Place the remaining cream cheese in a star-tipped pastry bag and pipe a decorative garnish around the torte. Top with a tomato rosette (see Garnishes, page 165). To serve, cut into wedges like a pie.

Confetti Cheese Wheel

Serves 12.

A colorful pastry wheel brimming with cream cheese-vegetable "confetti" can be prepared on short notice and served with confidence!

INGREDIENTS

2 pie sticks
2 ounces cream cheese
¼ cup sharp spreadable Cheddar cheese
2 tablespoons minced black olives
2 tablespoons minced pimiento
2 tablespoons minced chives
¼ cup chopped cooked ham

INSTRUCTIONS

1. Prepare pie sticks according to package directions. Roll out one pie stick to a 9-inch circle. Flute the edges and prick with a fork.
2. Roll out the other pie stick to a 7-inch circle. Flute the edges and score into 12 equal wedges, being careful not to cut all the way through the dough. Bake both circles on ungreased cookie sheets the time recommended on the package. Allow to cool.

3. In a mixing bowl, combine the cream cheese and Cheddar cheese. Whip until light and fluffy. Add the olives, pimiento, chives and ham. Blend thoroughly.

4. Spread the cheese filling smoothly and evenly to the edge of the 9-inch pastry circle. Top with the scored 7-inch circle.

5. Refrigerate until firm. To serve, cut into 12 equal pieces.

Caviar and Egg Wedgewheel

Yields 24 wedges.

Wedges of caviar and chopped egg complete this colorful wheel. Fashioned from just 6 slices of bread, this hors d'oeuvre is elegant, effective and best of all, tasty!

INGREDIENTS

½ cup butter, softened
¼ cup finely chopped chives
5 hard-cooked eggs, finely chopped
6 4X4 sandwich slices white bread, toasted
½ cup red caviar
Fresh parsley

INSTRUCTIONS

1. Spread 2 slices of bread with a thin layer of butter and a layer of caviar. Trim the crusts and cut into pattern #18.

2. Combine the remaining butter with chives and blend thoroughly. Spread the remaining bread slices with a layer of the butter mixture followed by a layer of chopped eggs. Trim the crusts and cut into pattern #18.

3. To assemble the wedgewheel, make a circle of caviar wedges, points angling outward, on a platter 12 to 14 inches in diameter.

4. Fit 2 egg wedges between each caviar wedge angling the points in. This makes a zigzag pattern.

5. Garnish the center of the wheel with sprigs of parsley. Refrigerate and serve chilled.

Roquefort Cheese Pie

Yields 10 to 12 wedges.

Tastes as good as it looks! A luscious layer of Roquefort and cream cheese spread over a pastry circle holds tasty bits of anchovies, eggs, green pepper and black olives encircled by a colorful ring of pimiento.

INGREDIENTS

1 pie stick
8 ounces cream cheese
4 ounces Roquefort cheese
2 ounce can flat anchovy fillets,
 drained and chopped
6 hard-cooked eggs, with yolks and
 whites chopped separately
½ cup chopped green pepper
Black pitted olives, sliced
Whole pimiento, sliced into thin strips

INSTRUCTIONS

1. Prepare the pie stick as directed on the package. Roll out dough to a 9-inch circle. Place on a baking sheet. Flute the edges, prick the bottom and bake as directed. Allow to cool.
2. In a mixing bowl combine the cheeses and blend thoroughly. Spread the cheese mixture evenly on the pastry circle.
4. Place the chopped anchovies in the center of the pie. Around the center, create concentric circles of chopped egg yolks, green pepper, chopped egg whites and olive slices. Finally rim the pie with the pimiento strips.
5. Refrigerate until firm. To serve, slice into wedges.

Caviar Cheese Pie

Yields 10 to 12 wedges.

This tasty "bull's-eye" sports a target of delectables. Caviar, cream cheese, eggs, onions and parsley are arranged on pie dough in graduated circles and served chilled.

INGREDIENTS

1 pie stick
8 ounces cream cheese, softened
¼ teaspoon garlic powder
1-ounce jar black caviar
8 hard-cooked eggs, with the whites
 and yolks chopped separately

INSTRUCTIONS

1. Prepare the pie crust according to package directions. Roll out to a 9-inch round resembling a pizza crust and bake on a baking sheet as recommended on the package. Allow to cool.
2. Combine cream cheese and garlic powder thoroughly. Spread a thin layer of the seasoned

½ cup chopped scallions
4-ounce jar red caviar
½ cup chopped parsley

cream cheese on the pie crust.

3. Arrange the black caviar on top of the cream cheese in a neat little circle in the very center of the pie. Around the caviar center arrange concentric rings of chopped egg yolk, scallions, red caviar, egg whites and finally parsley.

4. Refrigerate until firm. To serve, cut the pie into wedges.

Anchovy-Cheese Squares

Yields 12 squares.

Rows of color—mushrooms, egg yolks, cherry tomatoes and black olives—make this dish a beauty to behold. A base of cream cheese and anchovy makes it a delight to taste. And the instructions below make it easy to prepare.

INGREDIENTS

1 recipe Sour Cream Pastry, page 107
8 ounces cream cheese, softened
2 tablespoons mayonnaise salad
   dressing
¼ cup minced onion
2 tablespoons chopped anchovies
3 medium mushrooms, sliced
5 to 6 hard-cooked egg yolks, chopped
3 to 5 cherry tomatoes, cut in half
4¼-ounce can pitted black olives,
   chopped

INSTRUCTIONS

1. Preheat the oven to 350 degrees. Prepare pastry according to the instructions.

2. Roll out dough to a 9-inch square, ¼ inch thick. Bake on a flat baking sheet 15 to 20 minutes. Allow to cool.

3. In a mixing bowl combine cream cheese, mayonnaise, onion and anchovies. Blend all ingredients thoroughly.

4. Spread the cream cheese mixture on the cooled pastry square.

5. Mentally divide the square into 7 vertical rows, each approximately 1¼ inches wide. Arrange sliced mushrooms on the first row, chopped egg on the second, halved cherry tomatoes on the third and chopped black olives on the fourth. Repeat the sequence except for the row of olives. Chill.

6. At serving time, cut the square in half right down

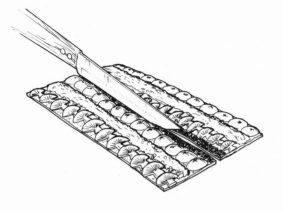

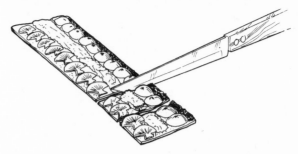

the center of the olive row. You now have 2 rectangles. Cut each rectangle horizontally into 6 equal slices and serve chilled.

CANAPÉ GAMES

We've all read about the games people play—These are games people eat! Canapés can form decks of cards, dominos, Mah-Jongg tiles. Whichever game you decide to play, the winning trick is a clever garnish and piquant butter. These canapés add a whimsical touch to card parties or other informal get-togethers. They may look intricate, but you'll find that with nothing more than a pastry bag, aspic cutters and a bit of culinary sleight of hand, you can create a festive hors d'oeuvre display that will certainly score with your guests.

Mah-Jongg Tiles

Yields 30 tiles.

INGREDIENTS

2 pullman slices or 8 4X4 sandwich slices egg or white bread, cut ½ inch thick

¾ cup butter, softened

3 tablespoons anchovy paste

16 ounces cream cheese

½ teaspoon garlic powder

4 hard-cooked egg yolks

½ cup tomato paste

INSTRUCTIONS

1. Combine the butter with the anchovy paste and mix well. Let stand at room temperature.
2. Prepare the spread by combining cream cheese and garlic powder.
3. Spread a thin layer of anchovy butter on the bread.
4. Next spread a generous layer of seasoned cream cheese on the butter.
5. Cut the bread into designs resembling Mah-

SPECIAL EQUIPMENT
Pastry bag with writing tip

Base: Egg or white bread
Butter: A blend of butter and anchovy paste
Spread: A combination of cream cheese and garlic powder
Garnish: A combination of egg yolk and tomato paste

Jongg tiles, pattern #4 for pullman slices and #12 for 4X4 slices.

6. Combine egg yolks and tomato paste for the garnish and place into a pastry bag with writing tip.

7. Pipe Mah-Jongg characters on each cut piece of bread. Refrigerate and serve chilled.

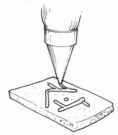

Caviar Dominos

Yields 30 dominos.

INGREDIENTS
¾ cup butter, softened
3 tablespoons finely chopped chives
2 pullman slices or 8 4X4 sandwich
   slices white or egg bread
1 8-ounce jar black caviar
4 ounces cream cheese, softened

SPECIAL EQUIPMENT
Pastry bag with writing tip

Base: White or egg bread
Butter: A blend of butter and chives
Spread: Caviar
Garnish: Cream cheese

INSTRUCTIONS
1. Combine the butter with the chives and mix well.
2. Spread a generous layer of the chive butter on the bread slices.
3. Next spread an even, thin layer of caviar over the butter.
4. Cut the bread into small rectangular shapes resembling dominos, pattern #4 for pullman slices or #12 for 4X4 slices.
5. Place the cream cheese in a pastry bag with a writing tip. Pipe tiny cream cheese dots on each "domino." And for that extra touch of authenticity, divide the "dominos" in half with a straight line of cream cheese.
6. Refrigerate and serve cold.

Playing Cards

INGREDIENTS

16 ounces cream cheese, softened
½ teaspoon garlic powder
¾ cup butter, softened
2 pullman slices or 8 4X4 sandwich
  slices egg or white bread
4-ounce can whole pimientos
½ cup tomato paste
4 hard-cooked egg yolks
3½-ounce can pitted black olives
4-ounce jar black caviar

SPECIAL EQUIPMENT
Pastry bag with writing tip
Aspic cutters

Base: Egg or white bread
Butter: Butter
Spread: Blend of cream cheese and
garlic powder
Garnish: Pimiento and tomato-egg
paste for red cards; olives and caviar
for black cards

INSTRUCTIONS

1. Combine the cream cheese and garlic powder. Set aside at room temperature.
2. Spread a thin layer of butter on the bread.
3. Spread a generous layer of the cream cheese mixture over the butter.
4. Cut the bread into rectangular shapes resembling miniature cards, using bread cut pattern #4 for pullman slices and #12 for 4X4 sandwich slices.
5. To fashion the red cards, cut shapes out of the whole pimientos with aspic cutters.
6. Combine the tomato paste and egg yolks. Place the mixture in a pastry bag.
7. Apply the tiny pimiento shapes onto the cream cheese. To make the numbers, pipe the tomato paste-egg yolk mixture on the corners of the cards.
8. To fashion black cards, flatten the black olives and cut tiny shapes with aspic cutters.
9. Apply the olive shapes onto the cream cheese and pipe numbers made from caviar on the corners of each card.
10. Refrigerate and serve chilled.

Backgammon Set

This board comes together in a matter of minutes, and so will your guests when they discover that everyone wins in this delectable game. Colorful wedges of caviar and cream cheese team to form a pip of an hors d'oeuvre. A bit of culinary whimsey, a sharp knife and a sense of humor is all you need.

INGREDIENTS

9 4X4 sandwich slices white bread, toasted
¾ cup butter, softened
4 ounces black caviar
4 ounces red caviar
16 ounces cream cheese, softened
2 ounces chopped anchovies or anchovy paste
3 hard-cooked eggs
Round crackers

SPECIAL EQUIPMENT
Egg slicer

INSTRUCTIONS

1. Trim the crusts from the bread slices.
2. Spread 4 slices of bread with a thin layer of butter. Cover 2 of the slices with a layer of black caviar. Cover the other 2 slices with a layer of red caviar.
3. Cut all 4 slices into pattern #19.
4. Combine the remaining butter with the anchovies and blend thoroughly. Spread a thin layer of the mixture on the remaining 5 bread slices. Cover with a layer of cream cheese. Cut 2 of the slices into pattern #14. Cut the rest of the slices into pattern #19.
5. To assemble the backgammon board, place 12 wedges of alternating colors beside each other with the points alternating. Repeat with another strip of 12 more wedges opposite the first, leaving a 3-inch space in the center (4 wedges of black and red caviar will be left over for nibbling).
6. Place a dividing strip of cream cheese rectangles down the center.
7. For an extra touch of authenticity, slice the eggs with an egg slicer and garnish the sides with "chips" made of egg slices atop crackers. Serve chilled.

Caviar-Egg Yolk Checkerboard

Yields 64 squares.

Realistic enough for a game! Delectable enough to eat! Alternating squares of caviar and egg yolk combine to form an edible checkerboard. Easy to prepare and fun to serve.

INGREDIENTS

16 ounces cream cheese, softened
½ cup anchovy paste
15 hard-cooked egg yolks
½ cup butter, softened
16 4X4 sandwich slices white bread,
    toasted
8 ounces black caviar

SPECIAL EQUIPMENT
Small mesh strainer

INSTRUCTIONS

1. In a mixing bowl, combine 8 ounces of the cream cheese with the anchovy paste and blend thoroughly.
2. Press the egg yolks through a strainer into a small bowl.
3. Spread softened butter on all of the toast slices.
4. Spread the cream cheese-anchovy mixture generously and smoothly on 8 slices of toast.
5. Generously apply strained egg yolks on top of the anchovy mixture with a spoon.
6. Spread remaining 8 ounces of cream cheese generously on the other 8 slices of toast.
7. Top the cream cheese with an even layer of caviar.
8. Trim the crusts from all the bread slices and cut them according to bread cutting pattern #12.
9. Arrange the squares on a flat platter, alternating the colors in a checkerboard pattern. Refrigerate and serve chilled. Garnish with parsley.

Fourteen

❧ Noshes

❧ Ah, such a chapter! Filled with traditional snacks worthy of being called noshes. What traditional gathering would be complete without some of these favorites. A nosh is traditionally something to munch on—a hearty snack, delicious fingerfood. Rich, flaky pastries filled with substantial blends of meats, cheeses, potatoes and other vegetables are nutritious offerings, whether dinner-sized or bite-sized party fare. The spices are light; flavors come from the foods themselves. Beware of calories in these innocent-looking hors d'oeuvres, and be sure to balance your assortment.

Chopped liver, blintzes and, of course, potato latkes are contained in this delectable chapter along with other traditional nosh favorites. There are even special Serving Suggestion Notes for those unfamiliar with noshes. So eat, my child, and enjoy!

DO-AHEAD NOTE

With the exception of the potato latkes, which are best when served fresh, these noshes may be prepared in advance, sealed tightly, and refrigerated or frozen. Serve them chilled or reheated, as indicated in the recipes that follow.

Eggplant Dip

This tangy eggplant dip is a delicious, low-calorie accompaniment to richer noshes like blintzes and chopped liver.

INGREDIENTS

1 medium to large eggplant
⅓ cup minced onion
3 tablespoons lemon juice
2 tablespoons olive oil
1 teaspoon sugar
Dash of garlic powder
Salt and pepper to taste

INSTRUCTIONS

1. Prick the eggplant once or twice with a fork and bake in a 475-degree oven for approximately 30 to 40 minutes, until the skin turns dark brown.
2. Allow the eggplant to cool until it can be handled. Peel off skin. Quarter eggplant and place in a food processor or blender. Add the onion, lemon juice, olive oil, sugar, garlic powder and salt and pepper. Process until smooth. Check seasoning.
3. Chill thoroughly before serving.

SPECIAL HINTS

When purchasing eggplant, look for firm, smooth skin that has a rich, purple color.

SERVING SUGGESTIONS

Serve the eggplant dip on a bed of fresh green lettuce surrounded by a ring of crackers.

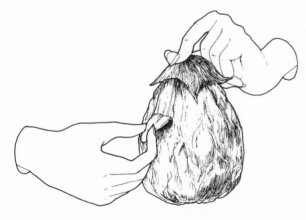

Lox Rollettes

What Sunday brunch is complete without smoked salmon? These small lox rollettes will make a big impression, as guests enjoy an innovative treatment of an old favorite.

INGREDIENTS

6 small white boiling onions
6 cherry tomatoes
½ pound smoked salmon
1½ cups whipped cream cheese

INSTRUCTIONS

1. Peel the boiling onions. Cut each onion and cherry tomato into 5 thin discs. Refrigerate until use.
2. Trim the lox slices into pieces approximately

1½X3 inches. (If the slices you have are not quite 1½ inches wide by all means use them anyway. These measurements are only guidelines. Save trimmings to mix with cream cheese for your own luncheon spread.)

3. Place approximately 1 generous teaspoon of whipped cream cheese at one end of the lox ribbon. Roll up the lox neatly.

4. Place a slice of onion followed by a slice of cherry tomato on top of the roll. Skewer them with a frilled toothpick.

5. Refrigerate until serving time.

SPECIAL HINTS

Select firm cherry tomatoes and thin slices of lox. Olives, pimientos or marinated mushroom caps make lovely alternative garnishes.

Chopped Herring Salad

Yields 2½ cups.

Served with pumpernickel bread, this sweet and sour variation on pickled herring is sure to become a new family tradition, one you can pass down through the generations.

INGREDIENTS

4 fillets of schmaltz herring
1½ medium onions, diced
½ cup diced sweet pickles
1 tablespoon white vinegar
1 tablespoon sugar
1 teaspoon vegetable oil

SPECIAL EQUIPMENT
Food processor or blender

INSTRUCTIONS

1. Soak the herring in water overnight in the refrigerator.

2. Place the herring along with the onion in a blender or food processor. Chop, but do not allow to overprocess into a puree.

3. Transfer the chopped herring and onion into a mixing bowl and add the remaining ingredients.

4. Gently stir the entire mixture for 3 to 5 minutes to distribute the flavors evenly.

5. Chill for several hours before serving.

SPECIAL HINTS

The chopped herring salad should have a fairly thick consistency for easy spreading.
Fillets of herring can be purchased in jars and tins in the supermarket or fresh at the deli.

SERVING SUGGESTIONS

Serve this salad well chilled in a glass bowl and, for an extra gourmet touch, place the bowl in a mound of crushed ice to keep the herring cold. Have plenty of spreaders conveniently arranged near a tray of buttered pumpernickel triangles.

Potato Latkes

Yields 30 latkes.

A customary treat during Chanukah, this old favorite can be served as an hors d'oeuvre when made in convenient silver-dollar-sized rounds. Delicious when served with a dollop of sour cream, applesauce and a light sprinkle of cinnamon, latkes are welcome anytime of the year.

INGREDIENTS

2 eggs
1 medium onion, diced
2 large potatoes, peeled and cubed
2 tablespoons flour
¼ teaspoon salt
⅛ teaspoon ground black pepper
Vegetable oil for frying
1½ cups sour cream
1½ cups applesauce
Cinnamon

SPECIAL EQUIPMENT

Blender or food processor

INSTRUCTIONS

1. In a blender or food processor, combine the eggs, onion, potatoes, flour, salt and pepper. Blend until smooth.
2. Heat approximately ¼ inch of oil in a skillet. Drop 1½ to 2 tablespoons of the batter into the hot oil to form silver-dollar-sized rounds.
3. Fry until brown on one side, then flip the latkes over and fry the other side.
4. Drain the latkes thoroughly on paper towels. Serve hot with sour cream, applesauce and cinnamon.

DO-AHEAD NOTE

Though latkes are best when served hot off the stove, they can be made slightly ahead of time and kept warm in the oven.

Chopped Liver

Yields 2 cups.

It's considered the mainstay of many a wedding. I've even heard it said that a wedding shouldn't take place without it. Though I can't assure eternal marital bliss, I can assure that chopped liver will keep your guests content. Reliable and always welcome, this spread can be molded to suit any occasion.

INGREDIENTS

1½ pounds chicken livers
2½ medium onions, diced
3½ tablespoons rendered chicken fat*
4 hard-cooked eggs
Kosher salt
Freshly ground pepper to taste

SPECIAL EQUIPMENT

Food processor or meat grinder
2-cup mold

INSTRUCTIONS

1. Sauté the chicken livers and onions in 2 tablespoons of the chicken fat.
2. Remove the liver and onions from the skillet with a slotted spoon, allowing the liquid to drain off.
3. Process the livers, onions and remaining ingredients in a food processor until smooth or put through the fine blade of a meat grinder. For an especially smooth consistency, add 1 extra teaspoon chicken fat and process again.
4. Lightly oil a 2-cup mold and add the chopped liver, packing it firmly and evenly.
5. Refrigerate until serving time, reserving just enough time to unmold and garnish.

SPECIAL HINTS

Vegetable oil may be substituted for chicken fat, if you prefer.
This recipe makes 2 cups, but it can be doubled or tripled successfully to accommodate your particular mold.

ARTIST'S NOTE

Decorate the top of the unmolded chopped liver with egg yolk or tomato roses and a few leaves of fresh mint or parsley sprigs.

SERVING SUGGESTIONS

Serve the chopped liver molded or sculpt it into your favorite shape.

*Rendered chicken fat can be purchased in many butcher shops.

Kasha Rolls

Yields approximately 24 slices.

Kasha roll, a flaky pastry just like mama used to make, is filled with a sumptuous blend of kasha (buckwheat groats) mushrooms and onions. Such an hors d'oeuvre!

INGREDIENTS

½ cup kasha (buckwheat groats)
2 eggs, beaten separately
1 cup boiling water
½ cup chopped onion
5 large mushrooms, chopped
½ cup plus 3 tablespoons margarine
Kasha Roll Pastry (below)
1 beaten egg plus 2 tablespoons ice
 water for "egg wash"

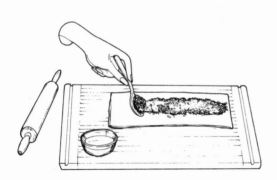

INSTRUCTIONS

1. Preheat the oven to 450 degrees.
2. Prepare the filling first. Combine the kasha and one beaten egg in a saucepan. Heat the mixture, stirring until the kasha grains separate.
3. Add boiling water, stirring the mixture well while pouring. Cover and simmer for approximately 30 minutes until kasha is soft, stirring occasionally.
4. In a separate pan, sauté the onion and mushrooms in 3 tablespoons of the margarine until the onion is soft. Add to the kasha mixture.
5. Melt the remaining margarine and blend it into the kasha mixture along with the second beaten egg. Mix thoroughly. Let stand until cool.
6. While the mixture cools, prepare kasha roll pastry and roll out as directed.
7. Place 6 tablespoons of kasha filling in the center of each of the unbaked pastry rectangles. Roll the dough around the filling, jelly roll fashion, forming two 12-inch rolls. To seal the roll, moisten the exposed end of the dough and press down firmly.
8. Place the rolls seam side down on a lightly oiled baking sheet. Brush rolls lightly with egg wash.
9. Bake in preheated oven for approximately 20 minutes, until the crust is golden brown.
10. Cut the roll into 1- to 1½-inch-wide slices and serve hot.

Kasha Roll Pastry: Combine 2 cups flour, ⅔ cup plus 2 tablespoons vegetable shortening and 1 teaspoon salt. Add ¼ cup ice water very slowly, mixing while you pour. Divide the dough in half and roll each portion into 12X6-inch rectangles, ¼ inch thick.

DO-AHEAD NOTE

Kasha rolls are best when served hot. Bake them just before serving time and keep them hot on a heating tray.

Potato-Onion Fingers

Yields 30 fingers.

Rich and piping hot right out of the oven, these vegetable fingers will have you licking your own. Potato and onion are the foundation of this hearty baked hors d'oeuvre.

INGREDIENTS

1 cup diced onions
¼ cup rendered chicken fat*
2 cups mashed potatoes
½ cup potato flour or potato pancake
  mix
1 egg
Salt and pepper to taste
Red horseradish (optional)

SPECIAL EQUIPMENT
Pastry bag

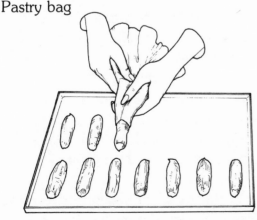

*Rendered chicken fat can be purchased at many butcher shops.

INSTRUCTIONS

1. Preheat the oven to 375 degrees.
2. Brown the onions in 3 tablespoons of the chicken fat. Let them cool slightly.
3. In a mixing bowl combine the mashed potatoes, potato flour, egg, salt and pepper.
4. Add the browned onions and remaining 1 tablespoon chicken fat to the potato mixture and knead well.
5. Fill a pastry bag without a tip with the potato mixture.
6. Squeeze fingers approximately 2 inches long onto a greased baking sheet.
7. Bake in preheated oven for approximately 20 minutes. Serve the potato fingers hot alongside a container of red horseradish for dipping.

DO-AHEAD NOTE

Prepare the fingers a day ahead of time and refrigerate them on a baking sheet. Bake the fingers just before serving time.

Blintzes

The well-known blintz is so versatile that it's appropriate for any gathering at any time of day. Vary the size to suit your purpose: small and dainty for bite-sized hors d'oeuvres or large and filling as a meal or side dish.

INGREDIENTS

Cheese Filling or Meat Filling (recipes below)
4 eggs
2 cups milk
2 tablespoons sugar
½ teaspoon salt
2 cups presifted flour
Butter
Oil for frying (optional)

SPECIAL EQUIPMENT
Blender or food processor
5-inch skillet

INSTRUCTIONS

1. Prepare the filling of your choice in the morning or a day ahead of time and refrigerate.
2. Beat the eggs well in a blender or food processor. Add the milk, sugar and salt. Gradually add the flour by spoonfuls for a thin, smooth batter.
3. Lightly grease the bottom of the skillet with butter and place over medium-high heat. When the butter is hot but not burning, pour about 2½ tablespoons of batter into the pan, just enough to make a very thin pancake. Tip the pan to cover it completely with batter.
4. When the pancake is lightly brown on the underside, turn it out, brown side up, onto a plate.
5. Repeat the procedure, lightly greasing the skillet each time, until all the batter has been used.
6. Fill each pancake brown side up with 1 tablespoon of cheese filling or meat filling in the center. Fold over the pancake sides and roll them up. (See crepe illustration, page 128)
7. Fry the blintzes several at a time, to a golden brown, in a small amount of oil, or bake them at 425 degrees until brown.

Cheese Filling: Combine 2 cups farmer-style cheese, 2 tablespoons large-curd cottage cheese, 1 teaspoon vanilla, 1 egg, 2 tablespoons sugar and 1 tablespoon grated orange rind (optional).

Meat Filling: Combine 2 cups chopped cooked beef or chicken, ½ cup chopped onion, ½ cup chopped green pepper, 1 beaten egg and salt and pepper to taste.

SPECIAL HINTS
When frying blintz batter, keep in mind the resulting pancake should be thin and flexible.

DO-AHEAD NOTE
Prepare the blintzes several days in advance. Store them unfried and well covered in the freezer. Fry or bake them just before serving.

SERVING SUGGESTIONS
Blintzes are best when served hot, so serve them soon after frying or keep them heated in the oven. Top the cheese blintzes with sour cream, yogurt, fruit preserves or your favorite prepared pie filling.

Fifteen

❧ Mousses, Dips and Patés

❧ For those who enjoy the elegant offerings of a buffet table, these mousse, dip and paté recipes are designed especially for you.

Mousses: These mousses offer a variety of taste, color and design. They can be chilled in a wide range of molds, from large and elaborate shapes that are unmolded onto a large chilled platter garnished with fresh greenery, to tiny nut cup molds turned out onto crispy toast rounds. Whatever your choice of molds, the taste and color will be refreshing and inviting.

Dips: At home with the most elaborate of buffets, these recipes offer an especially elegant twist to dips. For these dips are served hot! Chunks of seafood, cheeses and spices are blended to a bubbling richness.

Patés: The famed paté offers an air of gourmet elegance to any buffet and lends itself especially well to garnishes of all types. The elaborate yet deceptively easy paté included here is sure to bring praises, for it is a feast for the eyes as well as the palate.

DO-AHEAD NOTE

With the exception of the hot dips, which are best prepared just before serving, mousses and patés can be prepared in advance and refrigerated until serving time.

156

Crabmeat Mousse

Yields 2-quart mousse.

Generous on the king crabmeat, this luxurious mousse is elegant enough to serve the most dignified guest. Chill it in a mold and serve it cold. Then bring out the champagne!

INGREDIENTS

3 envelopes unflavored gelatin
½ cup cold water
¾ cup mayonnaise
¼ cup lime juice
3 tablespoons chopped chives
3 tablespoons chopped parsley
3 tablespoons prepared mustard
6 cups flaked king crabmeat
¼ cups heavy cream, whipped

INSTRUCTIONS

1. In a small saucepan or stainless steel bowl, soften the gelatin in cold water. Place over low heat to dissolve the gelatin.
2. Remove from heat and stir in mayonnaise, lime juice, chives, parsley and mustard. Mix well. Add the crabmeat and stir until combined.
3. Gently fold in the whipped cream and place in a lightly greased 2-quart mold.
4. Chill until firm. Unmold and serve.

Tuna-Cucumber Mousse

Yields 5½-cup molded mousse.

A light and refreshing hors d'oeuvre that's simple to make and particularly welcome in hot weather. Tuna and shredded cucumber are blended with a creamy dressing, chilled in a mold and served on an ice-cold bed of lettuce.

INGREDIENTS

2 envelopes unflavored gelatin
¼ cup lemon juice
1 cup boiling chicken broth
1 cup mayonnaise
½ cup milk
2 tablespoons minced scallion
2 teaspoons dill
½ teaspoon pepper
2 cans (7 ounces each) tuna, drained
    and flaked
1 cup shredded cucumber

INSTRUCTIONS

1. Combine gelatin and lemon juice in a mixing bowl. Let stand until gelatin softens. Add the broth and stir to dissolve the gelatin.
2. Add the mayonnaise, milk, scallion, dill and pepper. Chill approximately 30 minutes or until slightly thickened.
3. Beat gelatin mixture until frothy. Blend in the tuna and cucumber.
4. Pour into lightly oiled 5½-cup mold and chill until firm.
5. Place on a bed of lettuce and serve cold.

Petite Salmon Mousse

Salmon served with finesse! This heavenly mousse is molded in tiny nut cups, placed on toast rounds and artfully garnished with olives, tomatoes or pimiento.

INGREDIENTS

1 cup flaked salmon
2 tablespoons chopped scallion
2 teaspoons dill
2 tablespoons lemon juice
1 cup chicken broth
1 cup sour cream
1 envelope unflavored gelatin
45 Toast Rounds (recipe below)

SPECIAL EQUIPMENT

45 nut cups, 1¾ inches in diameter, or a 3½-cup mold.
2-inch round cookie cutter

INSTRUCTIONS

1. In a blender combine salmon, scallion, dill, lemon juice and ¾ cup of the chicken broth. Blend until smooth. Stir in the sour cream.
2. Soften gelatin in remaining ¼ cup chicken broth in a small saucepan. Stir over a low heat until the gelatin is dissolved.
3. Stir the gelatin mixture into the salmon. Blend thoroughly.
4. Brush the nut cups lightly with oil. Fill each with the salmon mixture, set on a tray and chill until firm.
5. Unmold the tiny mousse tarts on 2-inch toast rounds. Garnish with olives, tomatoes or pimiento.
6. Keep refrigerated until serving time.

Toast Rounds: Toast 23 slices white bread, spread lightly with softened margarine. Cut 2 2-inch rounds from each toast slice with a cookie cutter.

SERVING SUGGESTIONS

If you've used a 3½-cup mold, unmold onto a bed of lettuce and garnish with tomato roses and pimiento-stuffed olives.

Hot Lobster Dip

Yields approximately 3½ cups.

Tiny chunks of lobster blend with peppers and cheese create an incomparable dip that will lend elegance to any hors d'oeuvre table.

INGREDIENTS

3 tablespoons butter
1 small onion, finely chopped
½ cup diced green pepper
¼ cup diced red pepper
8 ounces processed cheese spread
16½-ounce can lobster meat, drained and flaked
2 teaspoons Worcestershire sauce
1 teaspoon pale dry sherry
¼ teaspoon pepper
3 tablespoons catsup

INSTRUCTIONS

1. In a double boiler, melt the butter. Add the onion and cook until soft.
2. Add the green and red peppers and the cheese. Cook, stirring until the cheese melts to a buttercream consistency. Add the lobster meat, Worcestershire sauce, sherry, pepper and catsup. Stir until all ingredients are well blended.
3. Serve hot in a small chafing dish or container that can be kept warm.

Hot Crab Dip

Yields approximately 4½ cups.

For magnificence of flavor and sumptuous blend of ingredients, this dip is hard to match. Tender bits of crab combine with cream cheese, mustard, onions and sherry to form an absolutely delectable sauce.

INGREDIENTS

16 ounces cream cheese, cubed and softened
½ cup mayonnaise
1 tablespoon prepared mustard
1 tablespoon minced onion
1 clove garlic, minced
¼ cup pale dry sherry
2 cups fresh or frozen crabmeat, drained and flaked

INSTRUCTIONS

1. In a double boiler, heat the cream cheese and mayonnaise. Stir until the cream cheese is melted.
2. Add the mustard, onion, garlic, sherry and crabmeat. Stir until all ingredients are well blended.
3. Serve hot in a small chafing dish or container that can be kept warm.

Liver Paté in Bread

Yields 10 to 12 slices.

An unusual twist on the very elegant paté en croute, this paté is served in bread. Topped with jellied consommé and garnished with olives and pimiento, this ordinary bread loaf transforms into a most impressive package. Just chill, slice and serve!

INGREDIENTS

1 envelope unflavored gelatin
10¾-ounce can beef consommé
½ cup plus 3 tablespoons butter, softened
8 ounces cream cheese, softened
1 medium onion, minced
1 pound chicken livers
3 tablespoons brandy
2 cloves garlic, finely chopped
1 teaspoon dry mustard
Salt and pepper to taste
1 pullman loaf bread, unsliced
2-ounce jar pimiento-stuffed green olives
2-ounce jar pimiento strips

SPECIAL EQUIPMENT
Blender or food processor

INSTRUCTIONS

1. Dissolve gelatin in cold consommé. Heat the mixture, stirring gently, until gelatin is completely dissolved. Cool, then refrigerate until the consommé is partially jelled.

2. Whip ½ cup butter and the cream cheese together. Let stand at room temperature.

3. Melt remaining 3 tablespoons butter in a skillet. Add onions and livers. Sauté over medium heat until livers can be easily cut with a spoon but are still slightly pink inside. Add brandy and heat until the mixture bubbles. Cook over high heat for 1 minute, stirring, to reduce liquid in skillet.

4. Drain off any liquid remaining in pan. Place the liver mixture into a blender or food processor. Add the garlic, mustard and salt and pepper. Puree until smooth. Add the butter-cream cheese mixture and process until thoroughly blended. Refrigerate 1 hour.

5. Make a rectangular or diamond-shaped cavity in the bread loaf by slicing ½ inch from the top and hollowing out the inside, leaving a ¾-inch border all around. Trim crust off sides.

6. Fill the bread with the paté, leaving a smooth surface. Fill to the top with partially jelled consommé and decorate with olive slices and pimiento strips.

7. Brush a film of the remaining consommé around the outside of the bread and garnish with more olives and pimiento.

8. Refrigerate at least two hours. Slice thinly and serve chilled.

Sixteen

🌿 Salads

🌿 Here are the fillings and accompaniments to many of the recipes in this book. You probably have your own favorite recipes for these salads, which, of course, you may substitute in the amounts called for. But if you don't and would like to add some new ones to your salad repertoire, you'll enjoy these.

Pineapple-Chicken Salad

1½ cups finely chopped cooked chicken
⅔ cup crushed pineapple, well drained
⅓ cup mayonnaise
¼ cup chopped walnuts
Combine all ingredients and mix well. Yields 2¾ cups.

Turkey Salad

1½ cups diced cooked turkey
1 cup finely chopped celery
½ cup mayonnaise
½ teaspoon prepared mustard
Salt and pepper to taste
Combine all ingredients and mix well. Yields approximately 2½ cups.

Coleslaw

1¾ cups finely shredded cabbage
¼ cup shredded carrots
⅓ cup mayonnaise
2 tablespoons sugar
1 tablespoon vinegar
½ teaspoon celery seed
½ teaspoon mustard
¼ teaspoon salt
Toss the cabbage and carrots together. Combine the mayonnaise, sugar, vinegar, celery seed, mustard and salt and mix well. Add the dressing to the cabbage and carrots and toss. Yields approximately 2 cups.

Tuna Salad

2 7-ounce cans tuna, drained and flaked
½ cup diced celery
½ cup diced onion
2 tablespoons sweet pickle relish, drained
2 to 3 tablespoons mayonnaise
½ teaspoon salt
Freshly ground pepper to taste
Combine all ingredients and mix well. Yields 2 cups.

Egg Salad

6 hard-cooked eggs, diced
1 teaspoon chopped pimiento
2 tablespoons chopped scallion
1½-2 tablespoons mayonnaise
½ teaspoon salt
¼ teaspoon freshly ground pepper
¼ teaspoon paprika
Combine all ingredients and mix well. Yields 2 cups.

Guacamole

2 ripe avocados, peeled and mashed
½ cup diced onion
1 tablespoon sour cream
1 teaspoon garlic powder
½ teaspoon lime juice
¼ teaspoon chili powder
Pinch cayenne pepper
1 cup chopped tomatoes (optional)
Combine all ingredients and blend well. Yields approximately 2 cups.

Ham Salad

1½ cups ground, cooked ham
⅓ cup minced celery
2 tablespoons sweet pickle relish, drained
¼ cup mayonnaise
1 tablespoon minced pimiento
½ teaspoon ginger
½ teaspoon marjoram
Combine all ingredients and mix well. Yields approximately 2 cups.

Macaroni Salad

2 cups cooked elbow macaroni
½ cup sweet pickle relish, drained
¼ cup diced American cheese
¼ cup diced green pepper
¼ cup chopped ham
2 tablespoons mayonnaise
Combine all ingredients and mix well. Yields approximately 2 cups.

Potato Salad

1 cup cooked cubed potatoes
2 hard-cooked eggs, diced
½ cup diced onion
½ cup cooked peas
2 tablespoons sweet pickle relish
2 tablespoons mayonnaise
1 teaspoon mustard
Freshly ground pepper and salt to taste
Combine all ingredients and mix well. Yields a little over 2 cups.

Marinated Eggplant

1 medium eggplant—baked, peeled and
   diced
½ cup diced green peppers, lightly sautéed in
   1 tablespoon butter
½ cup chopped onions
½ cup tomato paste
8-ounce can pitted black olives, sliced in half
1 teaspoon Worcestershire sauce
1½ tablespoons olive oil
1 large clove garlic, minced
1 tablespoon vinegar
½ teaspoon celery seed
½ teaspoon sugar
½ teaspoon salt
½ teaspoon garlic powder
Pinch of ground coriander
Freshly ground pepper to taste

Combine all ingredients and mix well. Yields approximately 4 cups.

SPECIAL HINTS
Prick the skin of the eggplant and bake 40 minutes at 450 to 475 degrees. Remove the skin and dice the eggplant.
Refrigerate the prepared salad for at least 1 hour before serving.

Seventeen

🌿 Garnishes

🌿 The garnish is the artist's signature, and adds the special touch that transforms hors d'oeuvres into individual works of art. A turn of a knife, a twist of a vegetable, and an ordinary cucumber becomes a flower. A slice of ham transforms into a rosebud, and olives furnish its simulated leaves and flowerpot.

Garnishes need not be elaborate to be effective. The simplest of garnishes thoughtfully applied add an impressive accent of color and interest. In this chapter are some tricks of the trade and sparks for the imagination. There are many garnishes from which to choose, and once you've had a chance to try a few, you may be tempted to come up with a design or two yourself. The elements are simple and the results masterful!

Scored Lemon and Cucumber

To score decoratively, cut long strips of peel along the length of the fruit or vegetable with a zester.

Tomato-Cucumber Twist

Score the cucumber with a zester and cut a thin slice. Slice a firm tomato of the same approximate size. Place the tomato slice on top of the cucumber. Make a small slice halfway through both and twist both ends simultaneously in opposite directions.

Cantaloupe Twist

Peel and cut a small cantaloupe into quarters. Shave a thin slice from one of the wedges with a paring knife. Twist the ends in opposite directions.

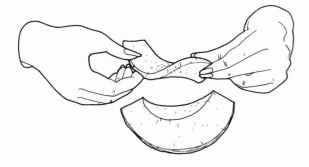

Salami Rose

Three thin slices of salami and a toothpick are needed to fashion this rose. The larger the diameter of the salami, the larger the rose. Roll the first slice into a tight cylinder. Fold the second slice loosly around the cylinder. Holding the bottom edges firmly, wrap the third slice around the first two and fasten with a toothpick.

Note: These directions can also be used to fashion a cucumber rose.

Tomato Rosette

To fashion a tomato rosette, use a small to medium firm tomato. With a sharp paring knife, peel the tomato in a spiral from top to bottom, as thinly as possible for a realistic effect. Roll the peel inside out. (The outside of the skin will be on the inside.) Tuck the remaining end under, and you have a rosette!

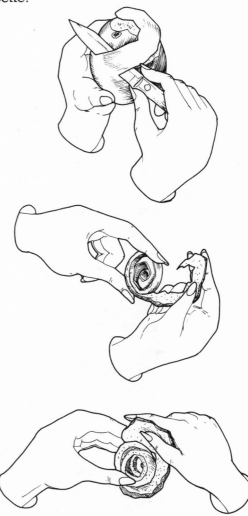

Crisscross Tomato Paste Pattern

Mix together 3 hard-cooked egg yolks and ½ small (6-ounce) can tomato paste. Fill a pastry bag with tomato-yolk mixture. Attach a writing tip and squeeze a crisscross pattern onto the spread.

Green Pepper Leaves

Cut a green pepper in quarters. Remove the seeds. Place it on a flat cutting surface. With a paring knife, carve leaf shapes to the desired size.

Carrot Slice Flowers

To form carrot slice flowers, slice the carrots thinly. Arrange 5 slices in an overlapping circular pattern to simulate petals. Accent with leaves fashioned from slivers of green olives.

Salmon and Ham Rosebuds

Tightly roll thin slices of ham and salmon jelly-roll fashion. With a sharp paring knife, cut the rolls into the recommended lengths. Cluster several of these tiny rolls on the spread. As they begin to unroll slightly, they resemble miniature rosebuds. Accent with leaves fashioned from olives.

Olive Leaves and Flowerpot

To make the olive flowerpot, cut an olive in half lengthwise, then cut one piece into a square. To form leaves and stems, cut a sliver from the remaining half for the stem. Cut the rest of the olive in two for the leaves.

Cheese Daisy Petals

To form a cheese daisy, cut 5 leaf shapes out of cheese slices using a leaf-shaped aspic cutter. Apply the individual cheese leaves in a circular pattern on top of the spread, forming a daisy. Dot the center with a caper or piece of black olive.

Piped Flowers

To fashion piped flowers, use a small pastry bag with the appropriate size star tip. Fill the pastry bag and twist the top. Squeeze while lightly pressing down. Lift up with a slight twist, leaving a star flower.

Mini Sweet Pickle Fan

To form a sweet pickle fan, thinly slice the pickle lengthwise. Cut just to the end but not all the way through it. Spread the slices, and you have formed a pickle fan.

Piped Shells

To form shells, fill a shell-tipped pastry bag. When piping shells in a row, simply squeeze and stop until you achieve the desired number of shells.

Eighteen

꧁ Gourmet Gadgets

꧁ In this section are found the gourmet gadgets used for creating our edible works of art.
Many of these gadgets are interchangeable and can even be improvised. By all means, do use your imagination to substitute gadgets and perhaps develop one or two of your own! All of the gadgets suggested here are not necessary for every recipe, so glance over the Special Equipment section before beginning, if you will, to see just which gadgets are suggested.

Cookie Cutters

Various shapes and sizes of cookie cutters are found in this group of gadgets. Many are simply metal circles of graduated dimensions, which can be purchased together. Convenient substitutes for some of these cutters are appropriate size glasses or cans. Cookie cutters are available at most grocery stores and specialty food shops.

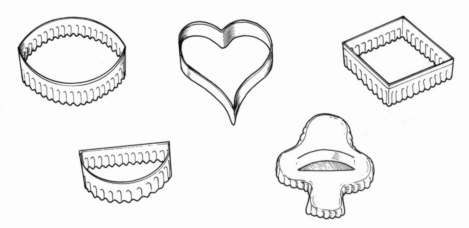

Cutters of various shapes: oblong, heart, diamond, crescent, clover.

Picks and Skewers

These handy wooden picks have a number of uses, ranging from convenient serving and handling of hors d'oeuvres to fastening tidbits. Or in the case of the cellophane-tipped toothpick, providing a bright display of color and festivity even for the simplest of preparations. Most of these picks are available at grocery stores or party shops.

Wooden skewers—6 inches long (sometimes called "tempura skewers")

Plain rounded toothpicks

Cellophane-tipped toothpicks

Tart Molds

Many different sizes and shapes of these delicate little containers are available. While specific sizes and shapes are suggested with recipes, tart molds can be interchanged for convenience and artistic preference. Tart molds are available at most cook shops.

1½-inch-diameter round tart mold

2½-inch-long boat-shaped tart mold

Oblong or round tart molds to 3 inches.

2-inch round tart mold

Flat-bottom tart mold 1 to 2 inches in diameter

Pastry Bag and Tips

Used for applying decorative designs, pastry bags are available in a variety of sizes. For our purposes a medium to small pastry bag is sufficient with the corresponding size tips. The pastry tips used most often for hors d'oeuvres are the star, writing and shell shapes. Pastry bags and tips are available wherever cake decorating supplies are sold.

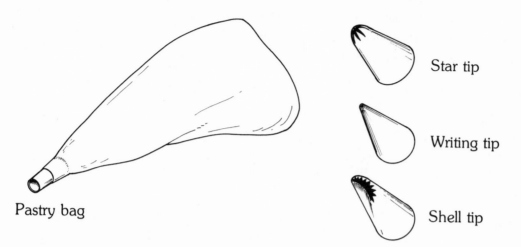

Pastry bag

Star tip

Writing tip

Shell tip

DESIGN CUTTERS

This particular group of gadgets is used for fashioning the actual designs, adding definition and character to our works of art. Available in most hardware stores and cook shops.

Aspic Cutters

Tiny metal shapes resembling miniature cookie cutters; used to fashion very small patterns.

Zester

Used for scoring and adding a decorative striped effect to fruits and vegetables.

Egg Slicer

Used to make uniform egg slices, for decorative purposes.

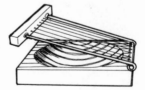

Sharp Paring Knife

Used for cutting and carving.

Ripple-Edged Knife

Used for slicing or peeling vegetables to give a decorative effect.

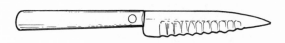

Pie Fluter

Wood, plastic or metal wheel usually used for cutting pastry and leaving a decorative imprint. Also used here for cutting cheese slices for that artful finishing touch.

CONVENIENCE GADGETS

These are the staples of our culinary tool chest, for they help speed and simplify. They are available at most department or cookware stores.

Blender or Food Processor

The modern-day magicians that make possible pureeing, grating and chopping in record time.

Strainer

Medium to small wire mesh is used here to strain egg yolks for garnishing.

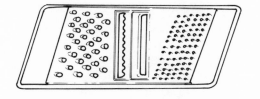

Melon-Baller

Used for fashioning balls from fruits and vegetables in two distinct sizes.

Shredder or Grater

Convenient to use when shredding or grating a small amount of cheese.

Garlic Press

Used to crush garlic cloves.

Spreader

A small knife having a wide, thin blade used for spreading evenly. Some spreaders have one serrated edge, leaving a design while spreading or cutting.

Pastry Brush

Used to coat pastry with egg glaze.

Wire Whisk

Handy for blending ingredients thoroughly.

Index